P9-CFZ-634

WITHDRAWN

New Albany – Floyd County Public Library

3 3110 00082 3987

Augustine

Twayne's World Authors Series
Latin Literature

Philip Levine, Editor

University of California, Los Angeles

TWAS 759

Augustine

By James J. O'Donnell

University of Pennsylvania

Twayne Publishers • Boston

Augustine

James J. O'Donnell

Copyright © 1985 by G. K. Hall & Company
All Rights Reserved
Published by Twayne Publishers
A Division of G. K. Hall & Company
70 Lincoln Street
Boston, Massachusetts 02111

Book Production by Beth Todesco
Book Design by Barbara Anderson

Printed on permanent/durable acid-free
paper and bound in the United States of
America.

Library of Congress Cataloging in Publication Data

O'Donnell, James Joseph, 1950–
    Augustine.

    (Twayne's world authors series. Latin literature; TWAS 759)
    Includes index.
    Bibliography: p. 140
    1. Augustine, Saint, Bishop of Hippo.
I. Title. II. Series.
BR65.A62O36 1985   270.2'0924   84–28133
ISBN 0-8057-6609-X

Contents

About the Author

James J. O'Donnell was raised in the shadow of the Saint Augustine Pass in the Organ Mountains of New Mexico. Educated by the Jesuits, he holds degrees from Princeton and Yale and has taught at Bryn Mawr College, the Catholic University of America, and Cornell University. He is at present associate professor and graduate chair in Classical Studies at the University of Pennsylvania. He is the author of *Cassiodorus* (1979) and post-classical editor of the *Bryn Mawr Latin Commentaries,* in which series he has published a commentary on the *Consolation of Philosophy* of Boethius (1984). His work on Augustine continues his investigations into the development of Latin Christianity, with particular emphasis on the interpretation of scripture and the spirituality that enacted that exegesis.

Preface

Augustine chose obscurity over ambition and labored a lifetime in a backwater without thought of making a name for himself. He died in an African city about to be overrun by invaders who spoke a German dialect and destined to be taken twice more in two centuries by other invaders speaking Greek and Arabic. All but the most trivial material traces of his life have vanished from the earth, and the faith for which he lived is widely thought obsolete. He survives in the books he wrote, but he wrote so many of them that he was not long dead before people began to say that anyone who said he had read all of Augustine was a liar; he wrote most of those books in heated controversies now long grown cold. But through all the centuries since his death, he has always had faithful disciples and outspoken adversaries.

Today Augustine is variously neglected, misunderstood, and taken for granted; but those who would understand our heritage cannot afford to pass over him lightly. This book is for those who care to look at the man squarely and to let his thoughts live anew, even if fleetingly. Those who read this book will, no less than its writer, fail in the desperate effort to bring a dead man back to life, but failure of this sort can be glorious and inspiriting. The effort requires no further justification.

But is there not already an immense literature on Augustine? Cannot any serious library provide the curious reader with whole shelves of books about Augustine, written from every conceivable point of view? So it might seem, but much of the more accessible work is now out of date and the specialized literature is largely dense, technical, and unavailable in English. The need remains for an introductory guide, to open doors and suggest paths to follow. That is the aim of this book.

We know more about the details of the life and career of Augustine than about any other figure from antiquity; we have not only the autobiographical data supplied by the *Confessions,* but also an abundant collection of his letters, supplemented by his books, many of which throw light on the circumstances in which they were written.

The first chapter is thus only a sketch of what we know, and concentrates on placing Augustine in the context of his native Africa.

The bulk of this book is then devoted to exposition of four segments of Augustine's gigantic oeuvre. The works discussed here make up about one-tenth of the verbiage of the surviving works. Little here will reflect the mighty labors of scholars in our time who have traced the development of Augustine's thought from earliest youth to maturity; rather, the emphasis is on the mature achievement of the bishop. To grasp that alone is matter for more than one book. The loftiest of his theological achievements, his long and difficult work on *The Trinity*, I have left reluctantly to the side: that book is best approached only after the kind of preliminary explorations sketched here have been completed.

The second chapter therefore surveys fundamental principles at the center of his thought, taking as text Augustine's first literary effort as bishop. His *Christian Doctrine* is the center of that discussion of both the main points of dogma to which he assented and the principles that guided his elucidations and explorations of those dogmas and their application to practical life.

The third chapter turns then to consider the implications of Augustine's beliefs for his view of human affairs in the perspective afforded by Christianity: the great book of his later years, *City of God*, provides a focus for those reflections. In the same years in which he was writing *City of God*, however, he was also embroiled in theological controversy with a much narrower focus on the relations of God with the individual soul. Thus our fourth chapter will take three controversial pamphlets from that controversy as the basis for an exploration of his ideas on grace, freedom, and the fate of man.

The last chapter of this book attempts to show the reader the way beyond Augustine's writings to Augustine himself. This attempt would be nonsensical had not Augustine himself conspired to facilitate the approach in his most important and beautiful book. In outward form, the last part of my study continues the pattern of the first parts, in that it introduces the reader to another of Augustine's works—the *Confessions*. Most modern readers coming to Augustine for the first time will want to read the *Confessions*, but without the earlier sections it would be very hard to present that text in any useful way.

For the *Confessions* happen to be a unique work, adroitly constructed by Augustine so as to efface itself and leave the reader to contemplate three things: God, the author created in God's image, and (neatest twist) the reader himself, created no less in the image of God than Augustine himself. This is sublime and subtle stuff, so artful that scholars still cannot agree on the plan but marvel at the success of its execution. My discussion tries to make the work accessible without glossing over difficulty.

It should not be concealed that Augustine can, to the casual reader, be difficult, even disappointing. He wrote believing that his own writings were worthless unless the same grace-driven conversion to the love of God that animated his own life was taking place in his readers. The reader who wants to avoid making life-transforming commitments merely to read a few old books should be warned that Augustine is going to be fighting him all the way. The guidance I hope to offer takes the reader's plight into account at every turn.

I owe a great deal to a succession of teachers, friends, and students, who have goaded me to read harder and interpret more clearly; and to Augustine.

James J. O'Donnell

Bryn Mawr, Pennsylvania
26 February 1984

Chronology

Chapter One
Augustine the African

Augustine was born in Tagaste (modern Souk Ahras, Algeria) in 354 and died almost seventy-six years later in Hippo Regius (modern Annaba) on the Mediterranean coast sixty miles away. In the years between he lived out a career that seems to moderns to bridge the gap between ancient pagan Rome and the Christian Middle Ages. But to Augustine, as to his contemporaries, that gap separated real people and places they knew, not whole imaginary ages of past and future. He lived as we do, in the present, full of uncertainty.

Augustine's African homeland had been part of Rome's empire since the destruction of Carthage five hundred years before his birth. Carthage had been rebuilt by Rome as the metropolis of Roman Africa, wealthy once again but posing no threat. The language of business and culture throughout Roman Africa was Latin. Careers for the ambitious, as we shall see, led out of provincial Africa into the wider Mediterranean world; on the other hand, wealthy Italian senators maintained vast estates in Africa which they rarely saw. The dominant religion of Africa became Christianity—a religion that violently opposed the traditions of old Rome but that could not have spread as it did without the prosperity and unity that Rome had brought to the ancient world.

Roman Africa was a military backwater. The legions that were kept there to maintain order and guard against raids by desert nomads were themselves the gravest threat to peace; but their occasional rebellions were for the most part short-lived and inconsequential. The only emperors who ever spent much time in Africa were the ones who had been born there; by Augustine's time, decades had passed without an emperor even thinking of going to Africa.

Some distinctly African character continued to mark life in the province. Some non-Latin speech, either the aboriginal Berber of the desert or the derelict Punic the Carthaginians had spoken, continued to be heard in dark corners. In some of the same corners old local pagan cults could still be found. When Augustine became a Christian clergyman, he found Africa rent by an ecclesiastical schism that had its roots at least partly in the truculent sense of difference maintained by the less-Romanized provincials of up-country Numidia, near the northern fringes of the Sahara.

So a young man like Augustine could belong irretrievably to the world Rome had made, but still feel that he was living on the periphery of that world. Augustine set out to make himself more Roman than the Romans and to penetrate to the center of the culture from which he found himself alienated by his provincial birth. But that was only the beginning of his story.

Augustine was born on 13 November, A.D. 354, in Tagaste, a town large enough to have its own bishop but too small for a college or university.[1] His parents, Patricius and Monica, belonged to the financially imperilled middle class. They were well enough off to have educational ambitions for their son, but too poor to finance those ambitions themselves. The fourth century was an age of mixed marriages at this level of society, in which devout Christian women like Monica were often to be found praying for the conversion of their irreligious husbands. Her prayers were not unavailing; Patricius accepted baptism on his deathbed. Though Patricius offered no direct impulse toward Christianity for his son, he must not have been much more than a passive obstacle.

Of Augustine's childhood we know only what he chooses to tell us in the highly selective memoirs that form part of the *Confessions*. He depicts himself as a rather ordinary sort of child, good at his lessons but not fond of school, eager to win the approval of his elders but prone to trivial acts of rebellion, quick to form close friendships but not always able to foresee their consequences. He studied Latin with some enthusiasm but never loved Greek. While he was leading what he wants us to think was a rather conventionally boisterous adolescence (it is best to imagine him in a crowd of conformists, but edging towards the quieter fringes of the crowd), his parents were worrying about paying for his education. Finally, with the help of an affluent family friend, they managed to scrape together enough to send him to the nearest university town a dozen miles away, Madaura, the home of the famous second-century sophist and novelist Apuleius, which was the second city in the life of the mind in Africa.

After a time at Madaura, the youth's talents made Carthage inevitable. He seems to have gone there at about the age of seventeen. Not long after, his father died and his mother was left with modest resources and nothing to tie her to Tagaste. Augustine himself quickly set up housekeeping with a young woman he met in Carthage, by whom a son was born not long after. This woman would stay with Augustine for over a decade and, though we do not know her name, he would say that "when he had to give her up to make a society marriage in Milan "his heart ran blood" with grief as she went off to Africa—perhaps to enter a convent. The son, Adeodatus, stayed with Augustine until premature death took him in late adolescence.

So far the conventional outward events of Augustine's young manhood. His intellectual life was a little more remarkable. The education he had received in Tagaste and Madaura had made him a typical late Roman pedant, with a comprehensive knowledge of a few authors (especially Cicero and Vergil) and a taste for oddities of language and style.[2] Only at Carthage did his education show any signs of breaking the usual molds, but even then only in a conventional way. In the ordinary course of the curriculum he had to read a work of Cicero's called the *Hortensius*.[3] This book, since lost and known only from fragments quoted by Augustine and other ancient writers, was a *protreptic,* that is, a treatise designed to inspire in the reader an enthusiasm for the discipline of philosophy. Through all his other vagaries of interest and allegiance, until the time of Augustine's conversion to Christianity Cicero would remain the one master from whom the young African learned the most; Augustine is in many ways the greatest of Cicero's imitators in point of Latin style.

The zeal for philosophy led first in what may seem a strange direction. Fired with the love of wisdom from his reading of the quintessential Roman politician, Augustine immediately joined a religious cult from Persia that had planted itself in the Roman world as a rival of Christianity: Manicheism. This sensual but sensitive young man, brought up around but not exactly in Christianity, took his Ciceronian enthusiasm with the utmost seriousness on the moral plane. He knew his own life did not in fact match his noble ideals. He was torn between the conventional pleasures of adolescence and the conventional rigors of philosophy. For this tension, Manicheism offered soothing relief. Augustine was not to blame that he felt this way, the Manichees told him, for he was only the pawn of greater forces that could, because Augustine was lucky and clever, be propitiated. Security could be had without sacrifice, and guilt removed without atonement.

The world the Manichees imagined was torn between two contrary powers: the perfectly good creator and the perfectly evil destroyer.[4] The world seen by human eyes was the battle ground for their cosmic conflict. The Manichees and their followers were the few who were on the side of the good spirit and who would be rewarded for their allegiance with eternal bliss. In the meantime all sorts of misfortune might befall the individual, but none of the wicked things he found himself doing were his fault. If the devil does compel sin, then guilt does not ensue. A few Manichees, the inner circle, were said to live perfect lives already, but the claim was hard to verify since the many disciples were kept busy waiting on the perfect few hand and foot, to keep the few from being corrupted by contact with the evil world of matter. The many were thus kept on a leash with easy promises and a vague theology.

Augustine was too clever to settle for vague theology for long. His most poignant moment of disillusion is recounted in the *Confessions,* when he finally met Faustus, the Manichee sage who would (Augustine had been promised) finally answer all the questions that troubled Augustine. When the man finally turned up, he proved to be half-educated and incapable of more than reciting a more complex set of slogans than his local disciples had known.

But while Augustine soon dissented privately from the Manichees, he did not break with them publicly. Even when he had decided the slogans were nonsense, they still provided the assurance that all the evil in Augustine's life was not his own fault and could not be let go of easily. Augustine associated with Manichees who thought he was one of them as late as 384, more than a decade after his first involvement with the sect.

Once initial enthusiasm faded, Augustine's attention drifted from the niceties of metaphysics to the realities of his career, which preoccupied him through his twenties. At about age twenty-one, after four years or so in Carthage, he went back to his home town to teach. He could well have stayed there forever, but his talent encouraged him to entertain loftier ambitions. He left again the next year.

From this decisive return to Carthage can be traced a career to which the adjective "brilliant" scarcely does justice. Seven years in Carthage matured the young teacher into a formidable scholar and orator. Education in a university town like Carthage at that time was a free-market enterprise, with each teacher setting up independently around the city center to make a reputation and inveigle students into paying for his wares; it was a competition in which many young men like Augustine must have fallen by the way. Augustine prospered, however, for when he became unhappy with conditions there (the students were rowdy and tried to cheat the teachers of their fees), he could think only of one place to which to move—Rome.

Rome of the fourth century was no longer a city with political or military significance for the Roman empire, but nobody at the time dared say such a thing. By common consent, the pretense was maintained that this was the center of civilization—and so the pretense became self-fulfilling prophecy. Academic prestige, the emptiest of glories, is a matter of reputation rather than reality; Rome had a reputation stretching back for centuries. Understandably it took Augustine a few months to find a place there, but when he finally found his feet, he could not have done better.

Some Manichee friends arranged an audition before the prefect of the city of Rome, a pompous and inept pagan named Symmachus, who had been asked to provide a professor of rhetoric for the imperial court at Milan.[5] The young provincial won the job and headed north to take up his position in late 384. Thus at age thirty, Augustine had won the most visible academic chair in the Latin world, in a period when such posts gave ready access to political careers. In the decade before Augustine's rise another provincial, Ausonius of Bordeaux, had become prime minister in the regime of a teen-aged emperor whose tutor he had been.[6] Our estimate of Augustine's talents is based largely on his later achievements; but that judgment together with his swift climb to eminence as a young professor makes it safe to assume that if Augustine had stayed in public life, he would have found very few limits to his advancement.

Augustine saw his prospects clearly. When his mother followed him to Milan, he allowed her to arrange a good society marriage, for which he gave up his mistress. (But then he still had to wait two years until his fiancee was of age and promptly took up in the meantime with another woman.) He felt the tensions of life at an imperial court, lamenting one day as he rode in his carriage to deliver a grand speech before the emperor that a drunken beggar he passed on the street had a less careworn existence than he.

Thus the strain of rapid advancement began to tell. His old perplexities rose again to plague him. He had tried Manicheism and it had failed; he owed some allegiance to Cicero, but in his day Cicero stood for little more than style and skepticism. He settled for ambivalence and prudent ambition. He had been enrolled as a catechumen (prebaptismal candidate) in the Christian church by his mother when he was a child; he acknowledged this status publicly (it was good for his career) to conceal anxiety and doubt.

His mother was there to press the claims of Christianity, but Augustine could probably have held out against her will alone indefinitely. Because, however, Monica was in Milan, and because Augustine was in public life and needed connections, he was soon caught between her and the most influential man in Milan, the bishop Ambrose. At first their encounters seem to have been few and perfunctory, but soon (due regard for his career probably required it) Augustine began to sit through a few of the bishop's sermons. Here Christianity began to appear to him in a new, intellectually respectable light. As before, his most pressing personal problem was his sense of evil and his responsibility for the wickedness of his life; with the help of technical vocabulary borrowed from Platonic philosophy Ambrose proposed a convincing solution for Augustine's oldest dilemma. Augustine had besides a specific objection to Christianity that only a professor of belles-lettres could have: he could not love the scriptures because their style was inelegant and barbaric. Here again Ambrose, elegant and far from barbaric, showed Augustine how Christian exegesis could give life and meaning to the sacred texts.

Resolution of his purely intellectual problems with Christianity left Augustine to face all the pressure society and his mother could bring to bear. More will be said below about the inner journey of his conversion, but the external facts are simple. In the summer of 386, not quite two years after his arrival in Milan, Augustine gave up his academic position on grounds of ill health and retired for the winter to a nearby country villa loaned by a friend in a place called Cassiciacum. He took along his family (son, mother, brother, and cousins) and friends, plus a couple of paying students who were the sons of friends. There they spent their days in philosophical and literary study and debate. Some of their conversations were philosophical and religious and come down to us in philosophical dialogues,[7] and we know that they spent part of every day reading

Vergil together. Though Augustine says he often spent half the night awake in prayer and meditation, the dialogues themselves are not dramatically theological. They seem to have been modest attempts to use the professional expertise of a rhetorician and philosopher to clarify technically the questions that had perplexed him. (The dialogues show a charming modesty about the powers of philosophical argument. In the midst of a long, abstract argument among the men, Monica would come into the discussion and in a few words, often quoting scripture, summarize an argument more clearly and concisely than the men had been able to do.)

In the spring of 387, Augustine and his friends returned to Milan for the forty days of preparation for baptism that preceded Easter. Then at the Easter vigil service on the night of Holy Saturday Augustine was baptized by Ambrose. Many people at that time, when Christianity was the fashionable road to success in the Christian empire, may have taken such a step casually and returned to their old ways, but Augustine was not one of them.

The great world of Rome had to be given up. Ambition now seemed hollow and sterile. Instead, Augustine and his friends decided to return to Africa, where they could still command a little property at Tagaste, to live in Christian retirement, praying and studying scripture. For a time their return home was held up by military disorders: a usurper came down out of Gaul and killed the emperor who resided at Milan, with ensuing disruption to the ordinary flow of commerce and travel in the western Mediterranean. While Augustine's party was at the port of Ostia near Rome, waiting for a boat back to Africa, Monica died.

Augustine returned to Africa at about the same age at which Dante found himself in the dark wood—thirty-five, halfway to the biblical norm of threescore and ten. He settled down at Tagaste in 389 with a few friends to form what we call, somewhat anachronistically, a monastery; it was probably very like the household at the villa at Cassiciacum in the winter of 386–87, but without the Vergil. Augustine would gladly have stayed there forever.

But such talent and devotion could not be left alone. Two years later, while on a visit to the coastal city of Hippo Regius, he found himself virtually conscripted into the priesthood by the local congregation. He broke into tears as they laid hands on him in the church and his fate became clear. Cynics in the audience thought these were tears of ambition and disappointment at not being made

bishop straight off, but they were only tears of deeply felt inadequacy. Augustine had for some time been avoiding cities that needed
bishops in fear of just such a fate.

He soon enough accepted his fate. He asked his new bishop,
Valerius, for a little time to prepare himself for his duties. Now,
if not before, he devoted himself to the mastery of the texts of
scripture that made him a formidable theologian in the decades to
come. His first expressly theological treatises come from this period,
devoted mainly to attacking the Manichees he knew so well. (Not
only did his experience make him an astute critic of the cult, but
it was politic for him to take a stand publicly, to thwart the inevitable innuendoes from other Christians that perhaps he had not
truly abandoned the Persian cult but was some kind of Trojan horse
sent to subvert the church.) His abilities were quickly recognized,
and by 393 he was being asked to preach sermons in place of his
bishop, who was a Greek speaker by birth. The old man passed on
in 395 and Augustine assumed responsibility for the church at
Hippo. He would remain at this post until his death thirty-five
years later.

Conventional accounts sketch Augustine's episcopal career in terms
of the controversies in which he took part. This brief sketch will
do likewise; but I must first point out the main inadequacy of this
approach. Augustine's first order of business through the decades
of his episcopate was the care of the souls entrusted to him. Most
of his life was an endless round of audiences with his clergy and his
people. He was constantly called upon to adjudicate all kinds of
disputes that had arisen in a world where the man of God was more
to be trusted as judge than the greedy magistrate sent from abroad
to represent Roman justice.[8] The real focus of his activity lay elsewhere still: the liturgy.

The early church was an institution centered upon the worship
of the community. Of a Sunday, every orthodox Christian in Hippo
could be found jammed into Augustine's basilica, standing through
a service that must have lasted at least two hours. We know from
the hundreds of sermons that survive how much care and imagination
Augustine put into preaching, tailoring his remarks to suit the
needs and capacity of his audience. The man who had been orator
enough to declaim for emperors must have been a spellbinding
preacher.

But even the homiletics of Augustine did not efface the dignity of the central act of worship. God was present on the altar for these people and this event was the center of Christian community life. Lukewarm believers in the throng attended out of respect for social pressure and a fear of divine wrath and were not much moved, but for Augustine, this was his central task. The controversies were only side-show, important only when they threatened to disrupt the unity of the community's worship.

But we know Augustine for his writings, and many of them were controversial. Three great battles had to be fought: the first was an ecclesiastical struggle for the very life of his community, the second a philosophical battle to effect the Christianization of Roman culture, and the last a theological quarrel of great subtlety over the essentials of faith and salvation. The first is the most obscure to moderns, while the second and third will be treated in more detail in the chapters that follow. Here we will concentrate on the ecclesiastical war that Augustine fought and won in his first decade and a half as bishop.

Donatism is the movement Augustine opposed, named after a bishop at Carthage some eighty years before Augustine's time at Hippo.[9] In those days the church had just recovered from the last bitter wave of persecution begun in 303 by the emperors Galerius and Diocletian. When fear subsided, Christians could breathe again and indulge in recriminations over the lapses of some of their number in time of trial.

The official position of the church was that those Christians who had compromised their religion in time of persecution could, with due repentance and atonement, be readmitted to full membership in the religious community. But there was a minority faction of enthusiasts who insisted that cooperation with the authorities in time of persecution was tantamount to total apostasy and that if any traitors wanted to reenter the church they had to start all over again, undergoing rebaptism. Evaluation of the credentials of those who sought reentry would be in the hands of those who had not betrayed the church.

The logical result of the Donatist position was to make the church into an outwardly pure and formally righteous body of redeemed souls. The orthodox party resisted this pharisaism, seeing in it a rigorism inimical to the spirit of the gospels. But Africa was known for its religious zealots and the new Donatist movement proved a resilient one. Even after official imperial disapproval had been expressed, the schismatic church continued to grow and prosper. By the time of Augustine's consecration as bishop, in fact, it looked as if the "orthodox" party was on the wane. In Hippo itself the larger church and the more populous congregation belonged to the Donatists in the early 390s. A constant state of half-repressed internecine warfare persisted between the communities. Popular songs and wall posters were pressed into service in the cause of sectarian propaganda. In the countryside, Donatist brigands ambushed orthodox travelers in bloody assaults.

Augustine began his anti-Donatist campaign with tact and caution. His first letters to Donatist prelates are courteous and emphasize his faith in their good will. He assumed that reasonable men could settle this controversy peaceably. But Augustine quickly discovered that reason and good manners would get him nowhere. In the late 390s, then, Augustine resigned himself to a course of action others in the church had long been urging: the invocation of government intervention to repress the Donatists. Augustine was dismayed at coercion in matters of religion, but consented to the new policy when he became convinced that the perversity and obtuseness of the Donatists were complete.[10] Even charity itself demanded that the Donatists be compelled to enter the true church in the hope that at least some would genuinely benefit from the change. They could not be worse off than they were.

Even when this policy had been settled upon, another decade of instability remained. Finally, in 411, an imperial commissioner conducted a detailed hearing into the facts of the matter, attended by hundreds of bishops from both orthodox and Donatist factions, and decided in favor of the orthodox party. From this time on Donatism was illegal and, though the schismatic community apparently showed some signs of life in remote parts of Africa until the Moslem invasions centuries later, the back of the movement had been broken, and at least the security and position of the orthodox party had been guaranteed.

The principle for which Augustine fought deserves emphasis. Christianity was not, he claimed, something external and visible; it was not to be found in obedience to certain clearly defined laws. Christianity was a matter of spirit rather than law, something inside people rather than outside. Most important, the church had room within itself for sinners as well as saints, for the imperfections of those in whom God's grace was still working as well as for the holiness of the blessed. Augustine drew the boundary of the church not between one group of people and another but rather straight through the middle of the hearts of all those who belonged to it. The visible church contained the visible Christians, sins and all; the invisible church, whose true home lay in heaven, held only those who were redeemed. Charity dictated that the visible church be open to all, not lorded over by a few self-appointed paragons choosing to admit only their own kind.

In A.D. 410, the city of Rome, with all its glories, was taken by barbarians under the leadership of the Visigoth Alaric. It is customary to say that shock waves ran throughout the Roman world at this event, but it is more correct to say that shock waves ran through those citizens of the Roman world prosperous enough to care about expensive symbols of Roman grandeur. A fair number of wealthy Romans fled the city to country estates in Campania, in Sicily, and in north Africa. Enough of them showed up in Hippo for Augustine to warn his flock that they should receive the refugees with open arms and charity.

Not long after the refugees settled on their African estates and began to frequent the salons of Carthage, the more intellectual among them began to wonder aloud whether their new religion might not be to blame for the disaster they had suffered. After all, the argument ran, Rome had been immune from capture for fully eight hundred years; but now, just two decades after the formal end of public worship of the pagan gods (commanded by the emperor Theodosius in 391), the city fell to the barbarians. Perhaps it was true what pagans had said, that the new Christian god with ideas about turning the other cheek and holding worldly empires in low esteem was not an efficient guardian of the best interests of the ruling class. Most of the people who indulged in these idle speculations were themselves Christian. The "paganism" of these people was no revival of ancient religion, but only the persistence of the ancient notion of religion as a bargain you struck with the gods in order to preserve your health, wealth, and complacency.

Augustine was invited by a friend, the imperial commissioner Marcellinus, who was in Africa to look into the Donatist quarrel for the emperor, to respond to these charges. He knew that it was more than a question of why Rome fell; here were Christians who still did not know what Christianity was about, how it differed

from the Roman religions it had replaced. His response was a masterpiece of Christian apologetics, *City of God,* whose composition
stretched over fifteen years. The first books, consoling those the
Visigoths had frightened, were published quickly and seem to have
done their job. But the work as a whole continued to come forth
in installments, revealing a broad vision of history and Christianity.

Marcellinus, a devout layman, also played a part in the last great
controversy of Augustine's life. One of the refugees from Rome had
been an unassuming preacher named Pelagius, who had stirred up
a moral rearmament movement at Rome.[11] Pelagius seems to have
appealed particularly to affluent ladies whom he urged to set an
example through works of virtue and ascetic living. He apparently
had a considerable effect for the good of the conduct of those with
whom he came in contact. But Augustine saw in Pelagius and his
followers an extreme position exactly opposite to the one he had
just rebuked in the cultured critics of Christianity, but one no less
dangerous. Pelagianism, as we shall see in more detail later on, was
theologically rather similar to Donatism, in that it assumed that
people could, by their own virtue, set themselves apart as the ones
on whom God particularly smiled.

Augustine never met Pelagius, though the latter had passed
through Hippo in late 410. Instead, he had to deal at all times
with the "Pelagians," the most notorious of whom, Caelestius, was
apparently a good deal less tactful and restrained than his teacher
had been. While Pelagius went off to the Holy Land, where he
became an unwilling center of controversy as he visited the sacred
sites, Caelestius and others back in Africa waded into the fray with
Augustine. Whatever the merits of the case, Augustine's side pre-
vailed in the ensuing scuffle. The authority of the papacy was invoked eventually—not without difficulty—and later that of the
ecumenical council of Ephesus in 431. Pelagius and his avowed
disciples were clearly and soundly defeated.

But the controversy did not end with the defeat of Pelagius.
Augustine had to face further questions, as the logical consequences
of the positions he took against Pelagius were examined by friend
and foe alike. Both in Africa and in Gaul, monks and their leaders
protested that the Augustinian theology of grace undermined their
own ascetic efforts in the cloister. In Italy, the young bishop of
Eclanum, Julian, engaged Augustine in a bitter debate that tainted
the last decade of the old bishop's life. A deep poignancy marks the

old man's dogged defense of himself and his belief against a young, resourceful, and resilient foe.

Old age and pressing concerns at home eventually delivered Augustine from the necessity of answering Julian. By 430, a band of barbarians had found its way even to Africa. The Vandals, who had first come from Germany into Roman Gaul in 406 and later passed through Gaul into Spain, had been invited into Africa by a Roman governor in rebellion against the emperor. The Vandals, like the Saxons later in the same century, proved to be deadly allies. In the summer of 430 they were besieging the city of Hippo as the aged bishop lay dying within. Shortly after his death they captured the city. Not long after, they captured Carthage and established a kingdom that lasted a century.

Chapter Two
Elements of Christianity

Augustine's elevation to the bishopric of Hippo in 395 gave him full powers to preach and teach in the church. Not long after, he characterized the bishop's life as one divided between looking after his flock, snatching a little rest where he could, and meditating on the scripture.[1] The last task was the most difficult and private: to preach and teach meant to proclaim the biblical message.

Conscious of his duty, Augustine soon began a work in four books on scriptural interpretation, which comes to us as his *Christian Doctrine*.[2] The first two books and part of the third were written c. 395/396, while the remainder was added c. 426/427, perhaps largely from notes and drafts retained from the earlier period.

Faith and Revelation

Just as an analysis of the use of language begins by using words of some kind, so an exploration of Christian theology begins with assumptions central to that theology. Augustine was conscious of these paradoxes, so *Christian Doctrine* begins with a dense and subtle book in which he makes his assumptions explicit. Since the purpose of this book is introductory, readers often pass through it briskly to get to the real business at hand, the manual of exegesis in Books 2 and 3, without penetrating the sophistication of thought and expression in this little *summa* of Christian teaching.

The starting point is deceptively simple and obvious. All teaching consists of two parts: things and signs (1.2.2). Theology makes certain claims, using the signs of language, about the things that make up reality. It begins with the metaphysical claim, to be explored in detail in the later books of *Christian Doctrine,* that language and reality can be securely related to each other in some way.

Every sign, of no matter what sort, is itself a thing. Semaphore gestures with the hands are just so much flesh in motion; language is just so much blast of wind; a printed text is just a curiously ornate arrangement of ink on paper. Before any sign can have meaning, it must be given that meaning by some reasoning being. Hence there is no watertight division between things and signs. Mark Twain's description in *Life on the Mississippi* of the complex language the riverboat pilot could read where laymen could only see ripples on the stream is a relevant parable of the conventional nature of language. For the purposes of this preliminary book, Augustine will concern himself with things insofar as they are things and leave the discussion of the interpretation of signs until later.

In this world, things exist as we encounter them. Augustine thus defines only two classes: the things that we enjoy and the things that we use (1.3.3). This, like the distinction between signs and things, is a purely utilitarian distinction and makes (for the moment) no metaphysical claims. Some things enter our consciousness as instruments by which other things may be obtained or affected— they are there to be used. Other things seem to have more final value, and are objects for which instruments are employed.[3] At first it is unclear whether Augustine intends any absolute distinction between classes of things or merely a distinction in our relations with things. For the most part, the latter seems to obtain. Things to be enjoyed themselves seem to fall into a hierarchy with a single highest good—enjoyed but never used—at the pinnacle.

But this ethical analysis will preoccupy us a little further on, after we have seen the theological use Augustine makes of his distinction. Suffice it to say for the moment that the distinction itself (like the distinction between things and signs) is purely neutral and does not point toward any particular value system. Augustine's purpose in these short opening chapters is to provide himself with a neutral vocabulary with which to describe basic Christian doctrine. Indeed, the whole of the first book is a tour-de-force for the way Augustine can use two simple a priori categories as the framework for a full and comprehensive theoretical description of Christian theology.

Even after we appreciate this, we are slightly unready for the abrupt statement that soon follows: "The things to be enjoyed are the Father, Son, and Holy Spirit, the very Trinity, one particular thing, the highest of things, the same to all who enjoy it" (1.5.5). Here the philosopher, who has appreciated Augustine's analysis and perhaps likened it to that of Kant, suddenly and urgently suspends his consent. So flat and arbitrary a statement as this prejudices all debate about the way values will be assigned using the thing/sign and use/enjoyment distinctions. Augustine knew this perfectly well;

the aim of this treatise, after all, was to discuss Christian doctrine. At some point, Augustine had to begin to speak of specifically Christian things. He was not one to do so in any tentative or questioning manner.

Two things need to be said about this assumption (some would say arrogation) of authority. First, when he wrote these words, Augustine spoke as a bishop of the Christian church, that is to say, as one of the direct successors of the apostles, with the same authority to preach and teach in the church as they had. He spoke, not out of any personal authority derived from superior wisdom and training, but out of the authority that came to him by virtue of his office. He could say what the church said with no diffidence at all.

Second, in due course he makes clear, as he describes the ways of God's intervention in the world, how it is that this ecclesiastical authority makes sense within the structure of Christian doctrine. But it must be admitted and emphasized that this work exists only within that structure. Augustine was never concerned with demonstrating the truth of the Christian religion entirely on the basis of principles accessible to the unaided human reason. As *Christian Doctrine* makes clear, divine revelation, that is to say, intervention in human affairs by a power anterior to all human reasoning, is the necessary condition of Christian theology. Perhaps when that revelation has done its work well, it might be possible to reconstruct the doctrines of Christianity as they would appear if the unaided human reason were in fact capable of devising them, but even in that case, only faith would make it possible to assent to that exercise of the rational faculty.

At any rate, Augustine is clear in stating where he begins: with the trinity. He lived at the end of a century that had worked out the church's basic trinitarian doctrines, at the ecumenical councils of Nicea in 325 and Constantinople in 381. Christians finally had a universal vocabulary in which to state what they believed about God, Christ, and the Spirit lucidly and concisely without error or imprecision.[4] Simple creeds are important as a foundation for a treatise such as this; when new candidates for church membership were instructed for baptism during the forty days before Easter, two themes predominated: introduction to the creed as a statement of the essentials of belief (all creeds were trinitarian in shape; what we call the Apostles' Creed was one of the most common) and introduction to the Lord's prayer as the prime medium of spirituality.

In a few chapters, Augustine then states the essentials of Christian belief in God, with a most important preamble: God is ineffable, that is, we can say nothing truly meaningful about one who transcends the categories of human language. Indeed, it is the wisdom of God that gives reasonableness to all things in human life. This feat is accomplished through the incarnation of the Word of God—and suddenly we have moved to the second person of the trinity. The mystery of incarnation is the nexus between God and man, by which, "though God himself is our home, for our sake he made himself the very road that would lead us home." A brief summary of the human life of Christ culminates with the resurrection and ascension (1.6.6–1.15.14).

What follows is an assertion that the church is the true body of Christ (1.16.15). What Augustine does not say so explicitly as we would like (but what would be obvious to his audience) is that in his discussion of the church we are meant to see the presence of the third person of the trinity, the Spirit. The foundation of the church at the first Pentecost consisted in the gift of the Spirit to the apostles gathered in the upper room. Viewed in this way, the three persons of the trinity represent God the unapproachable, God the mediator, and God the indwelling spirit. Knowledge, through revelation, moves down from above in this image, while human response moves back up from the church (body of Christ) to Christ (Word of God) to the ineffable godhead itself.

Here in a dozen pages, then, Augustine has laid out his assumptions. Since they arise from the teaching authority of the church he represented, his statement of them thus resembles in outline one of those simple baptismal creeds. But although he has presented this material in what seems to be a rather abstract and forbidding way, his is in fact a manner precisely suited to the development of his hermeneutical theory and practice in the following books. The second principal section of the first book of *Christian Doctrine* is devoted to a sketch of the implications of the distinction between use and enjoyment (1.22.20–1.34.38). This outline makes sense when seen as a statement of the way in which members of the church, the body of Christ, are to conduct themselves.

The fundamental principle persists in all its simplicity: human beings are to enjoy God. All other things and people they are to use.

To our ears this sounds crudely exploitative. We do not like to "use people." We have learned to appreciate the hidden costs of traditional social structures, and the self-seeking possibilities of apparent altruism. Can Augustine be rescued from a charge of cynicism? Perhaps.[5] He insists that what makes all the difference is the object toward which "use" is directed. We are rightly repelled when we see a man who "uses" people to aggrandize power and satisfy greed; in that case, the object toward which "use" is directed is the selfish interest of a single individual with no right to such advantage over his fellows and no sure intrinsic goodness or benevolence to lighten his rule.

For Augustine, the aim is altogether different. The center of all "enjoyment" is God—perfectly good, perfectly benevolent, perfectly reliable. God rules creation in somewhat the way that a playwright rules the stage, but God is much more firmly in control. God's goodness is so complete and perfect that dependence on his judgment and authority is completely without danger or risk. The behavior of petty tyrants in this world becomes, in Augustine's view, a vicious mimicry of divine governance, with some of the structure retained, but with all of the values perverted. What makes the difference is a good or bad object of "enjoyment."

Augustine envisions, moreover, a situation in which all "enjoyment" of ourselves is at least potentially ruled out. The goodness of God is so great and his judgment so reliable that the individual can abandon all self-will and self-directed exploitation once and for all. To say that Christians exploit others becomes then a special way of describing obedience to the second of the two great commandments of Christianity: "Thou shalt love thy neighbor." We are to love that which is good in our neighbors for the love of God, while hating what is evil, and to "use" ourselves in exactly the same relentless and uncompromising fashion. This kind of love sounds terrifying (perhaps "awesome" is a better word), but if it can be given perfectly, with exact perceptions of good and evil, it can lose all power to terrify. In like manner, something "terrific" always adheres to Christian descriptions of heaven, for heaven's is a life that knows nothing of the quirks, foibles, and small irrational attachments of human life in this world. The life described is one fit only for heroes—but promised to all. No longer is it as universally obvious as it once was that all men and women naturally desire such a life.

The Augustinian ethic reveals itself in practice as hierarchical. Proper use of all people and things requires an accurate assessment of their relative value in the plan of salvation. All right love is based on right knowledge. Order exists in nature, and only when order is perceived (that is, only when nature is seen as God created it and not merely as man imagines it) can the commandments of love genuinely be fulfilled. As Augustine puts it, "That man lives in justice and holiness who is an uncorrupted judge of things. He has an ordinate love and neither loves what he should not love, nor fails to love what he should love, or loves one thing more than he should, nor loves two things equally that deserve different loves, nor loves differently two things that deserve equal loves. Every sinner, insofar as he is a sinner, is not to be loved; but every man, insofar as he is a man, is to be loved on account of God. God is to be loved on account of himself" (1.27.28).

The implications of the Christian idea of love that was preached throughout Europe for over a thousand years deserve to be drawn a little more clearly. First, ordinary self-love is put in its place. Men are part of a whole larger than themselves and their needs and wants cannot dictate values to the whole. They have responsibilities, even to themselves, to recognize that this is so and to refrain from asserting private advantage at the expense of others—and even where others would not be hurt. The seven deadly sins (pride, avarice, lust, envy, gluttony, sloth, and wrath), even if committed in perfect solitude, do harm to the sinner. (A system of this kind takes the individual seriously in a way that one which merely counsels that we refrain from harming others cannot. This quality of the Augustinian system deserves to be called democratic.)

Second, love of fellow man appears in new light. The romantic love that was invented in the Middle Ages and glorified in the modern world runs a risk of going astray, for when the love of one person for another becomes all-consuming and exclusive, it begins to resemble idolatry (the medieval authors who toyed with the notion we call courtly love still knew this) and becomes a kind of false religion. When the lover's praise of his mistress flirts with hyperbole, it is forgiveable, but when the hyperbole begins to be taken seriously, some derangement has occurred.

Third, this view of love is profoundly communitarian. In a system in which every person voluntarily knows and accepts his or her place in the ordered pattern of society and acts for the best interests of

every other member of that society and of the society as a whole at
all times, a theoretically perfect life is in view. The medieval world
could both attempt to establish such a system on earth and yet
accept the inevitability of failure through sin; the modern world
either tries to establish such a utopian system (under a variety of
dictatorial regimes) or else (under more liberal regimes) refuses to
believe that such a system is even possible—both systems pervert
the democratic ideal by carrying it to excess. True love of neighbor
eschews grand schemes that attempt to impose one person's views
on others and contents itself with doing what is possible. "We
ought to hope all men love God with us" (1.29.30), Augustine
says, and explains by a homely example. Consider, he says, the
devoted fan of some theatrical celebrity and how he loves everyone
who shares his enthusiasm—not for the sake of those who share the
enthusiasm, but for the sake of the star they all admire; and consider
how he labors ceaselessly to spread his enthusiasm far and wide; and
how he loathes with a special passion anyone he finds who is in-
different to the charisma of the beloved. In parody this is how God
and man could behave toward one another, on condition that man
truly understood and accepted the perfect goodness and desirability
of God.

At this point in *Christian Doctrine,* Augustine inserts what looks
like a digression on the relations of men and angels (1.30.31–33).[6]
Augustine stresses certain features of the picture he has just drawn
by making us consider it *sub specie aeternitatis,* and so he draws us
for a moment out of the morass of imperfect human society and
bids us consider heaven. Will we still love our neighbor in heaven?
Yes, but in a much different way; for there, our neighbors will no
longer need our help to draw near to God, and our love will concentrate itself much more directly on God himself. This shows how
much the sinfulness of human life makes love of neighbor a more
rather than a less urgent command. Our fellow mortals are in a
state every bit as perilous as our own, at all times in danger of
eternal damnation and loss of God. In that light, their need for our
help becomes obvious and the legitimacy of conceiving love of neighbor in terms of the use/enjoyment distinction becomes more
intelligible.

The next section of Book 1 takes another unexpected turn. Suddenly Augustine is talking about how God does not enjoy us, but
rather uses us himself (1.31.34). First we began with God, then

saw the structure of divine involvement in human life, and now have been considering the human response to that divine gesture. Here in the last chapters of this part of the book we return to the point at which we began, considering the relation between God and man from God's point of view at last. This is a salutary reminder that Augustine's view of the world is resolutely theocentric, and that indeed if it were not so, we could easily charge him with hypocrisy. To take God's point of view as the most important is a logical consequence of the principles Augustine has been discussing in earlier chapters.

For since God is the central point of all that exists, God does not, in some half-hearted reciprocal way, treat us just as we treat him. He acts instead with what could be described as justified selfishness, making us the instruments of his own goodness and glory. God alone of all need not be humble. God is the source of all that is: insofar as men share in his being, they are good; insofar as men are evil, they decline to share that goodness and so earn punishment—which is, in the truest sense of the hackneyed phrase, "for their own good." When we love God and God loves us, we act in all ways in God, and thence comes all power to act for the good at all.

Hence a recapitulation of the themes of the book (1.32–35). First, the distinction between use and enjoyment gains new force from the finality of what has just been said about God; then, attention returns to the way that leads us home, that is, to Christ the mediator. Finally, Augustine confronts us with the crucial point of contact where theory becomes practice in the church animated by the spirit and, in particular, through the revealing act of God in scripture. A brief chapter is worth quoting in full:

> The sum and substance of all we have said here is this: let the reader understand that the whole aim and purpose of God's law and scripture is the love of that which is to be enjoyed [i.e., God] and of that which can enjoy along with us [i.e., neighbor]; for there is no need of a command to love ourselves. In order that we might know and do this, this whole ordering of the world for our salvation was accomplished by divine providence. We are to use the world, not with the love and delight we would show to our true home, but only with the passing love we would give a highway or the vehicles of travel. We love the things that carry us only because we love the place to which they carry us. (1.35.39)

This world, then, is not our true home. We belong with God. The world of creation is inferior to its creator and can only offer a temporary resting place. (Man is unique in the created world, for his soul, the thing that makes him special, is immortal and destined to persist even in the presence of God—that is one part of what it means to say that man is created in the image and likeness of God.) We are meant to live in this world as we would live in a foreign country. If we are truly citizens of the homeland we have left, we will pine for it, struggle to live according to its customs, and devote ourselves to making our way home. On that journey, we should not become so enamored of the inns and carriages that serve our journey that we give up the journey itself.

Human life, therefore, is transient. All that we touch passes away, and well it should; for all that we touch is good if it leads us home to God, but bad if it keeps us from him. The sweeping categorical effect of this principle cannot be minimized. As we shall see, Augustine is always aware that even the trappings and instruments of ecclesiastical office, which exist only to bring man closer to God, can themselves become instruments of damnation if he begins to love them for themselves.

The principle is universal. Though all things are potentially good (if used for the proper end), all things are potentially evil (if used for the wrong end, selfishly or idolatrously). Augustine is often suspected of an innate hostility to material creation, and this view is called (depending on the prejudice of the viewer) crypto-Manicheism or lingering Neoplatonism. The fact is that his suspicion, in the mature years after his conversion, had narrowed itself to focus upon the attitudes that people bring to material creation. If they treat it with due tentativeness, as something good for the moment but to be relinquished in a moment if love of God requires it, then both they and the things they touch are good and beautiful. But no matter how beautiful created nature is, it can become the focus for wrongful loves that lead people away from God. Then for those people, it is evil.

A more general point demands attention in this context. On the one hand, there are plenty of things that are intrinsically and objectively wrong to do; but at the same time (and the paradox of those last four words will come back to haunt us later), the intention with which men perform all acts (both those good and bad in themselves) is of everlasting importance. In making this claim,

Augustine seems to render absurd the usual categories of logical analysis. We will see time and again that such a taste for paradox is not incidental to Augustine's thought. Rather, he sees in many of the formal contradictions of human thought the persistent imperfection of the human mind. In Book 1 of *Christian Doctrine*, for example, he asserted the essential unity of knowledge and action by claiming that all right love (the only form of action that is morally justified) is based on and grows out of right knowledge, and at the same time claimed that right knowledge, which contains the command to love, is impossible unless united with right action in love. This theory unites faith with love, for faith is the one valid source of knowledge for fallen men, and love is the only acceptable moral response to that faith; but the combination of principles is a challenge to our usual logical categories. What Augustine is claiming is that the deepest of philosophical chasms, the distinction between subject and object, is itself an illusion born of sin and not an inherent quality of reality.

Modern physicists suspect that the observer cannot separate himself from the system he observes, but as heirs of the western philosophical tradition that goes back to Plato and Aristotle they have found it difficult to cope with the realization. The radical difference between Christian theology and that traditional western philosophy is nowhere more sharply defined than here. What Augustine says is that we cannot exist in the world simply as knower and observer. To do so is to condemn ourselves to a partial existence, imperfect and incomplete. The fullness of human life comes only when knowledge and observation are perfectly integrated with action and participation. The real Manicheism of our culture is that of the philosophical tradition that invented the distinction between mind and body—invented it because an imperfect world seems in practice to demand it, because men can in fact behave as though such a distinction were possible. Christianity turned away from that pessimistic habit of mind to claim that the semblance of division is only temporary and comes about as a result of our own actions, not of anything intrinsic in ourselves or the world.

Christian redemption is then the final healing of all the divisions that sin brings. Though spirit and flesh are at war with one another in the disorder of the fallen world, in the resurrection of the body they will be rejoined again in a harmony that Augustine insists once

existed. Better still, the deepest rift of all, between the eternal and
perfect creator and his mortal and sinful creations, will itself be
healed in the unity of the beatific vision. Evil itself will not merely
be vanquished; it will be seen never to have existed. All these
doctrines defy the power of fallen reason to comprehend or accept
them, for fallen reason itself is the source of the mutually contradictory categories that seem to make such ideas impossible. Christian
faith, while claiming to be ultimately in complete accord with
authentic reason, starts out as a scandal to reason, insisting we
believe pairs of contradictory propositions simultaneously. Only faith
can cross this divide; Augustine begins on the other side.

Scripture and Interpretation

Christianity is a religion of the book, but the book did not spring
out of a vacuum: hence the first book of *Christian Doctrine*. The
authority of the believing community precedes and guarantees the
authority of the book. Thus the Christian student of scripture brings
certain first principles along to the study of the book. The text
itself, like the church, is only an instrument of divine authority.
For both church and scripture the active agent of revelation is God,
working through Christ, the Word.

Though we have placed his preliminary discussion under a separate
heading, for Augustine the first book of *Christian Doctrine* was part
and parcel of his theory of interpretation, because acceptance of the
basic doctrines enunciated there was the foundation of all understanding of scripture. According to our way of thinking, the formally
hermeneutic part of Augustine's treatise begins only with the last
few chapters of Book 1, where the principles outlined are restated
to show their applicability to the study of scripture.

The beginning of all exegesis is love of God and love of neighbor.
"Whoever thinks he understands divine scripture or any part of it,
but whose interpretation does not build up the twofold love of God
and neighbor, has not really understood it. Whoever has drawn from
scripture an interpretation that does fortify this love, but who is
later proven not to have found the meaning intended by the author
of the passage, is deceived to be sure, but not in a harmful way,
and he is guilty of no untruth at all" (1.36.40).

Hence church doctrine makes it clear that all scripture will contain
the praise of this double love *(caritas)* and the condemnation of all

that is contrary to it—and nothing else. Here a special quality of a scriptural text is seen: in addition to whatever the initial writer meant to put into a text, there is also, always and everywhere, this deeper divine message. What is important, then, is that this deeper message be uncovered. This approach imputes a fundamentally instrumental quality to scriptural texts: God works on the individual soul through scripture, and however God works is good. Having a correct opinion about the meaning of an obscure word in scripture is a good thing, but ultimately irrelevant; but having a correct opinion about the need to love God and reform one's life is not only a good thing, but ultimately the only thing to be expected from scripture.

If love of God and of neighbor is the goal of interpretation, the enemy of interpretation is whatever does not allow that love to grow. The root of all lovelessness is the self-assertiveness of pride. The one who sets himself up as an authoritative interpreter of scripture in opposition to the reasonable suggestions of colleagues or the benign direction of the church goes far astray, even if he does uncover much arcane and accurate lore in the process. Not only is *caritas* the goal of interpretation, it is also the only reliable means of interpretation.

This is obviously a counsel of perfection. Augustine knew that all are sinners and all interpretations of scripture are imperfect, and he wanted to make sure the student of scripture knew it. All interpretation is tentative and incomplete; all the more reason why the only question that means anything is the one that asks whether the Word of God is acting in the reader's soul right now.

Charity abides, then. What passes away, for the interpreter of scripture, is the whole apparatus of interpretation, both practical and theoretical. But the purpose of *Christian Doctrine* is to provide all that apparatus. Augustine is at pains to make it clear that the apparatus is just that, a collection of instruments to be discarded when rendered obsolete. The reading of scripture itself, which the apparatus makes possible, is itself only a halfway measure. If text and interpretation become obstacles in the way of the goal, they are to be thrust aside and other instruments, even if less sophisticated ones, are to be found.

So Augustine's humble scholar opens the Bible and begins to read. How is he to proceed? To give order to his manual, Augustine uses a rough-and-ready division of the problems the exegete faces.

The categories are not in fact hard and fast, but rather represent two broad overlapping areas on a single spectrum. At any rate, the first book of *Christian Doctrine* enunciated Augustine's doctrine about things, so the remaining books deal with signs. In Books 2 and 3 Augustine deals with exegetical questions as such, distinguishing problems concerning signs of whose meaning one is ignorant ("unknown signs"—Book 2) from those concerning signs whose meaning is confused or unclear ("ambiguous signs"—Book 3). Both categories seem merely to deal with different degrees of ignorance, but Augustine is on to something a little more important here. In Book 2 he will deal with those signs whose meaning is conventional and uncontroversial and that can be made clear simply by the acquisition of readily available common knowledge (chiefly problems of text, language and historical context). In Book 3, however, he will approach the stickier questions of obscurity that come about when authors deliberately use signs in ways for which there are no conventional interpretations. Augustine's compartments are convenient, but not watertight.

Before treating unknown signs in detail, Augustine first plants the reader concretely in front of scripture itself and outlines some of its characteristic features—that is, its obscurities. Augustine on obscurity must be understood carefully. He sets no value on obscurity itself; rather, he sees obscurity as evidence of sin-darkened intelligence. The business of the exegete is to abolish obscurity, but Augustine does not claim to live in a perfect world. He accepts obscurity in scripture and is not unaware of the particular pleasures it brings. Just as he will say elsewhere that the fall of Adam was a *felix culpa* (happy fault) because it made possible the incarnation, so obscurity is the result of sin, but it provides opportunities for the redeemed intellect that would not be available otherwise.

The disentangling of obscurities is a matter of simple pleasure first of all. The mixture of obscurity and clarity in scripture is one way scripture adapts itself to the taste and preference of every audience. "This was undoubtedly arranged," Augustine says, "by divine providence to subdue pride with toil and to excite the understanding from the boredom it readily suffers solving similar problems" (2.6.7). To clarify his point, he gives an example.

Let someone tell me of holy and saintly men: the church of Christ draws on their strength and example to strip new converts of their superstitions and proposes them as models to imitate for those it incorporates into itself. The believers, good and true servants of God, shrug off the burdens of the world and come to the holy fount of baptism, coming up to bear fruit in the spirit of the twin love of God and neighbor. —So why is it that when I hear this spoken plainly and clearly, I know nothing of the special delight that comes when I read that passage in Solomon's Song in which the church in the figure of a beautiful woman is addressed: "Your teeth are like sheared sheep come up from the sheepdip, who all give birth to twins, and there is none barren among them." (2.6.7; Song of Songs, 4.2)

Remarkable enough to delight in teeth compared to a flock of reeking sheep, but harder still to accept that this passage of Song of Songs is to be interpreted as Augustine indicates. Granting him his reading for a moment though (we will have much more to say about that style in a few pages), one can see that his point is intelligible. The struggle to decipher a passage like the one quoted can certainly give the intellect a taste of its most characteristic pleasures; the game only seems jejune to the outsider. The obscurity of scripture, then, is bait for the learned and the wise, who might otherwise turn away if the entire text were simple and direct.[7]

And so the search begins. Augustine marks out seven steps to wisdom for the study of scripture to ascend. Wisdom begins with fear of God, which in turns becomes loyal obedience (for faith precedes understanding).[8] Both are passive qualities, acceptance rather than action. The turning point in the approach to wisdom is the third step: *scientia,* or knowledge (which, as we saw in the last section, is the basis of all right action), to which the study of scripture is an important (but not the only) contributor. Knowledge gives birth to strength, which is the source of good counsel, which leads to purity of heart, which is the final prerequisite to wisdom. Wisdom, then, is the result of both knowledge and action, faith and *caritas.* The opposites are all joined in unity. Wisdom can also be identified with divine wisdom, that is to say, Christ. This is in fact the ascent to Christ.[9]

The clarity and unity of Augustine's view of scripture study lets him turn from this theoretical statement of its nature and value to the most elementary of practical questions: what books does scripture contain? This was a pressing question in Augustine's time, because there was still no universal agreement on the exact number, division, names, and order of the books of the Bible. Manuscripts of the Bible were still in circulation that preserved orders and canons going back to early days; indeed, single complete manuscripts of the whole of the Christian scriptures were rare; when the whole was broken up in parts for convenience in handling, it obviously facilitated the loss of some parts and the mixing of versions of others. Augustine does not treat the Bible as a fixed and magical text sent down from on high: such an attitude would not match the vulnerable condition of the text as it came to him. He sees it as a document that draws its practical authority from the church. This does not mean that the church has independent authority, for the power to make such decisions is the power of the spirit. The test of the inspiration of scripture, then, is its recognition by the inspired church. This standard of selection is valid both historically (that is how in fact the canon of scriptures came to be: churches decided upon it) and theologically (the authority of both book and church is God's authority working in both).

Augustine's list is similar to that used today. The early church had gotten its Old Testament originally in the Greek Septuagint version made in Egypt before the time of Christ, and hence its canon includes the so-called apocryphal books, which do not occur in the Hebrew canon (and which were, for that reason, excluded by the early Protestant reformers). His New Testament is identical to the modern canon. [10]

Such is the outer form of the text. How is it to be read? First, a general knowledge of the contents should be obtained by thorough reading. What such a reading could be like is difficult now even to imagine. Augustine himself began serious study of scripture only after his thirtieth year, yet by the time he became a bishop in his early forties he could quote from memory from virtually every book of scripture at will. This is not to say that he had memorized the whole of scripture, but what struck him as significant he had little trouble committing to memory. This preliminary reading of scripture should let the reader absorb the principal ideas of the text in those passages where the message is simple and clear. With those ideas in hand the reader can proceed to face the obscurities.

The first obvious step is to learn the languages in which the scripture is written. Though Augustine himself was never more than a modestly competent Greek scholar and was completely innocent of Hebrew, he knew enough to admit his lacks and lament them. Where there are obscurities, the first step is to find out if they go back to the original text or not. (To obviate some of these problems,

Jerome compiled a handbook much used in the Middle Ages that gave the meanings of those Hebrew words occurring even in the Latin translations of scripture, mainly proper names.[11]) Augustine knew full well where the problems in the existing Latin translations came from: getting them translated from Hebrew into Greek was difficult and the task was performed infrequently, but from Greek into Latin was a different story: "In the early days of the faith, whoever came upon a Greek text of scripture and had some little facility in each language seems to have set himself to translating" (2.11.16). Understandably, this abundance of often only marginally competent versions could lead to much confusion.

Augustine deserves our sympathy and respect for his handling of language problems. In an ancient society where language was mainly a spoken idiom and any knowledge of reading and writing was comparatively rare, it was difficult to find someone who knew a language you wanted to learn well enough to teach it—and who was willing to stoop to the labor of teaching, a task usually left to professionals or slaves. No bilingual grammars or dictionaries existed. The problem was more acute still when a Christian sought to find a teacher for Hebrew: few learned Jews were willing to be much help. Faced with these obstacles, the most Augustine could do was express a pious respect for such competence in the alien tongues as could be found and then resign himself to making do with an obviously deplorable situation. What is remarkable is the considerable success that attended even these crippled labors. Luck, instinct, knowledge or parallel texts, and perhaps a little inspiration combined to make Augustine a more than decently competent interpreter of scripture by any standards.

After a brief summary of some working principles by which to judge translations (2.12–14), Augustine states his own preferences: in the Latin translations, he likes the so-called *Itala* version, while among the Greek versions he likes the Septuagint (2.15).[12] He was suspicious of the new version that his near-contemporary Jerome was producing in the desert near Bethlehem. Here, if anywhere, is where Augustine can be blamed for conservatism, but it must be remembered that people are always conservative about their versions of scripture. Throughout the Middle Ages, even after Jerome's revision became the basis of the so-called Vulgate, particular passages from the old translation with theological significance were remembered and quoted as authoritative, on the principle that nobody could tell for sure whether the theologically preferable (if linguistically obsolete) version could with certainty be eliminated.[13]

After some observations on the naturally figurative habits of language (for the remedy of which Augustine later wrote a book called *Figures of Speech from the Heptateuch*), he discusses at length the secular expertise that could be brought to bear on a text of scripture (2.16–39). He recognizes the utility of consulting the learned books of secular science for information to help understand a text of scripture. If scripture mentions a solar eclipse and you have never seen such a thing, a treatise on astronomy will undoubtedly be of use. But Augustine is mainly concerned here with warning his Christian readers of abuses that may arise from overhasty trust of secular authors.

History books, for example, are slippery witnesses. If they just contain a record of events, well and good; but only scripture contains a record of events from which a deeper meaning can be drawn. Natural science is useful, but astronomy particularly is to be handled with care, since in antiquity astronomy included most of what we call astrology. Augustine's concern is to make sure the reader understands that for the Christian there can be no other independent, self-verifying, nonsubjective source of knowledge besides divine inspiration working through the church and its scriptures. Omen and astrology are particularly to be avoided, but all abuse of the secular sciences is to be shunned.

This is a skeptical way of looking at secular wisdom, but there is another side to it all. Even philosophers, and especially the Platonists, can be read with profit—if proper care is taken. The biblical image Augustine invokes was popular among Christians considering the uses of secular wisdom. "Remember the Egyptians not only offered idols and terrible oppression, which the Israelite people hated and fled, but they owned vessels and ornament of gold and silver, and fine clothing besides, which the Israelites took for themselves in secret as they left Egypt, claiming it all for a better use" (2.40.60). The Christian student of scripture is to rob the Egyptians of their gold, taking what is valuable from secular authors and leaving behind what is idolatrous and useless.

But none of these practical remarks penetrates to the essence of scriptural interpretation. The prudent warnings of Book 2 could be directed with little change to anyone undertaking the scholarly study of a difficult text. For Augustine, however, scripture is not just a difficult text, and scriptural study not just a matter of scholarship. Book 3 of *Christian Doctrine* reaches the central questions.

So methodical is Augustine's mind that he is constantly impeded from getting to central issues by the need to deal with (to him) unavoidable preliminary questions. What about ambiguity that resists the application of specialized knowledge? First you must be sure you have read the passage correctly. Have you read it with the correct punctuation and deciphered its syntax correctly? (The ancient reader, confronted with a manuscript devoid of punctuation, required reading skill of a different order from what we need when we open our neatly printed books.)

Given these cautions, he is ready now to face fundamental problems of scriptural ambiguity. The most important principle is that thing and sign be adequately distinguished from each other. The literal meaning of a text (that is to say, its presentation of things as things plain and simple) should be respected, but the reader should be alert to detect any and all shifts into a more figural mode of speaking (when the things are also signs of something besides themselves). This may be technically imprecise, but it is still intelligible. Augustine is fond of these analytical distinctions (like thing/sign) that work in a variety of shifting contexts. A scriptural text is nothing but a collection of signs that are used to present things to our mind; but some of the things presented to our mind have further signifying power either in themselves or because the author has willed it so. Hence it makes sense to distinguish, within the signs of a text, between signs to be taken literally and signs to be taken figuratively.

Augustine had a scriptural basis for his undertaking. He quotes here (3.5.9) Paul to the Corinthians, "The letter kills, but the spirit gives life" (2. Cor. 3.6). In that quotation is a wealth of early Christian doctrine.[14] The Christian intuition is that all scripture is scriptural. If the Bible is the revealed word of God, then every word of the Bible is itself revelation. Paul naturalized the Old Testament as part of Christian scripture by insisting that the fullness of New Testament revelation could already be glimpsed, in a partial, evocative, and figurative way, through the Old Testament. The evolution of Christian biblical criticism is the working out of this principle. For the Greek world, Origen (c. 180–254) was the great master of the technique, while the chief Latin authorities (heavily dependent on Origen) were Augustine, Ambrose, and Jerome.[15]

The name of the method is allegory, and its traditional ancient definition is "saying one thing to mean another." In strictest sense, all reading is allegorical (when I read the word "horse" I understand the thing horse), but in fact the term limits itself to the use of language to carry a second meaning beneath the obvious surface. Christianity applies this principle to the whole of scripture, with the adventurous difference that it does not matter whether the author of the particular passage intended an allegorical meaning consciously or not. At bottom, only one story is told anywhere in scripture: the redemption of mankind by Christ. The story of David is an edifying tale (read in the literal sense) of God working in the world, but (in the allegorical sense) it also foreshadows Christ. The Song of Songs is a wedding song about ordinary mortals, but allegory instructs the Christian reader that the bride and groom can be taken as the soul and Christ, as the church and Christ, or even (in a popular medieval interpretation) as the Virgin and Christ.

This technique can readily be extended to almost any text: it almost becomes a parlor game. But for the early Christian church, including Augustine, it was serious business, for it was founded in scripture itself (cf. Gal. 4.21–31). Scripture was the proper subject of this treatment and—here is the central point—the literal, original sense of the passage must not be blotted out by the elucidation of allegory. Pagans had allegorized their own great works of literature when advances in philosophy left them embarrassed with the crudity of the classics. Thus they would claim that the *Odyssey,* for example, was only the story of the purification of a soul and its return to a heavenly homeland. What distinguished such interpretations from the Christian treatment of scripture was that the pagans ceased altogether to claim historical value for their subject text, admitting it to be mere myth or fiction. Christianity managed, combining opposites, to insist on the literal truth of the Old Testament narrative and on the allegorical significance of the narrative.[16] Book 3 of *Christian Doctrine* is Augustine's guide to allegory. But here, it is important to note, theory is more important than practice. Augustine is concerned not so much with giving his readers tools to work with as making sure they have the right motives and principles at the outset. Instruments will come to hand once readers are face to face with the scriptural text. But getting the one right answer does not count for much.

This may be a surprising claim to make about a Christian theologian seeking to interpret scripture, but it is true and illuminating. Augustine was not concerned with training schools of exegetes who would work independently and emerge with identical interpretations of the same passages; or who, if identical interpretations did not emerge, would work together in an atmosphere of mutual cooperation and inquiry until they had resolved their differences and agreed on a common line of reading. This would strike Augustine as a much too self-important way of going about the business of interpretation. Interpretations were not to be judged by any evanescent standard of objective accuracy in the natural order but by the absolute standard of orthodoxy and truth in the spiritual order.

In the practical order, what matters is the effect of exegesis. If an interpretation of scripture builds up *caritas* or (what amounts to the same thing) attacks its opposite, *cupiditas* (selfish desire), then it is, absolutely speaking, a good interpretation (3.10.15). As long as it is in accord with the rule of faith (*regula fidei,* which is in essence what Augustine outlined in Book 1), conformity to some external, but purely human, standard of correctness is immaterial.[17] In the grasp of eternal and divine truth, the exegete is left free to be as subjectively independent as he can be. A multitude of divergent interpretations may exist side by side without harm, as long as all meet the basic standards of building *caritas,* destroying *cupiditas,* and following the *regula fidei.* Conformity to *caritas* is conformity to the truth of heaven. The principle of the *regula fidei* insists that the belief of the entire Christian community is in itself the adequate practical guide. These two standards impose a considerable amount of what Augustine would recognize as objectivity on the subjective fantasies of the exegete. What matters is not the interpretation itself. The quality of the exegesis judged according to some professional, technical standard is irrelevant. What counts above all is the life of the believer who reads the scriptural text in the light of the interpretation. If the reader profits, the method is of little importance.

The reader will surely demand that certain minimum standards of fidelity to the text and plausibility are met, and that will exercise a further influence over the exegete. But it is for the exegete to know his own audience well enough to know what line of interpretation will help them most. Augustine still insists that the aim of any discourse is its persuasive effect on the reader, not conformity to a pretended standard of excellence and order.

After Augustine had outlined these basic principles of interpretation, he put *Christian Doctrine* aside for what turned out to be thirty years. From a point in Book 3 (at the end of 3.25.35), the work as we have it is a continuation made in the late 420s. With the end of the theoretical part of Book 3, Augustine had said all he had to say that was original and important about scriptural interpretation. Anything beyond that point would consist of actual interpretation itself, so directly did the theoretical principles point toward the act of reading itself. As we shall see very soon, the practical hints tacked on to the work at the end are of limited applicability, and some are obvious. What are we to make of the work's main line of teaching?

First, it constitutes the Augustinian statement of what is the most revolutionary thing about Christianity. Christianity does not merely depend on faith in God, it is that faith. Christianity asserts that there is another way to knowledge besides the ones sense and fallen reason discover for themselves. Moreover, Christianity claims that this other way is inaccessible to mankind's unaided efforts. But finally, Christianity asserts that, beyond all expectation, the eternal living God—the only being not affected by sin and the fall—has intervened in human affairs to make the better way accessible. So superior is that way and so intimately related to the life we should lead that to follow it is in itself salvation. The theological description of this, however open to conflicting readings, is "justification by faith alone."

In this world, this faith is manifest, above all, in Christ. Before Christ there had been intimations, and after him reactions; but Christ himself is the Word of God itself. His incarnation is the central act of revelation. Second to Christ in the worldly order, there is the church, endowed expressly by Christ with the authority of the spirit and, in Christ's absence, designated the arbiter of Christian doctrine. Third in order comes scripture, with the New Testament holding the key for a proper reading of the Old.

But finally there is nothing the church can do to guarantee that the message will reach those to whom it expounds scripture. The church cannot of itself give life to mere words—unless, says Augustine, grace intervenes to make it happen. The most the church can do is to try to keep the book (and itself) as transparent as possible. Hence the practical and self-effacing quality of *Christian Doctrine*.

Preaching and Teaching

But practical guidance is not worthless. In the conclusion Augustine added to Book 3 in 426/427, there is a list of seven rules for interpreting scripture, borrowed from a Donatist writer, Tyconius—a rare example of a patristic writer publicly acknowledging a debt to a member of a schismatic sect. Two things made it possible for Augustine to do this. First, the Donatist schism was no longer, in the late 420s, the pressing concern that it had been when *Christian Doctrine* was begun in the 390s. Second, Tyconius was not a typical Donatist and was, indeed, often in trouble with his own sect for ideas that brought him closer to the orthodox party.

Diffidence at naming Tyconius may have been part of the reason for deferring completion of *Christian Doctrine*. But my own opinion is that Augustine was daunted by the task of providing specific rules for the interpretation of scripture in practice (finding it, as I said before, easier to practice the art than lay down detailed guidelines), laid the work aside, and then came back to it and found it easier to add Tyconius's by no means useless rules than concoct new ones of his own. These rules can be taken several ways, but however read, they fall into two categories.

The simpler category is the most practical. Rules number four through six ("Of Species and Genus," "Of Times," and "Recapitulation") are the most "literary," dealing respectively with treatment of the figure of speech we would call synecdoche, with the symbolism of numbers, and with some quirks of narrative sequence.

The rest of the rules are more in step with the theological preoccupations of *Christian Doctrine*. The first rule, for example, "Of the Lord and His Body," incorporates a theology of the church on which Tyconius was much closer to the orthodox than to the Donatist view, drawing its inspiration from Pauline texts treating the church as the body of Christ. The second rule, "Of the Bipartite Body of the Lord," complements the first by treating two aspects of the church, that which is in the world intertwined with earthly society (and which appears as the visible church) and that which has already passed over to the afterlife.

When Augustine set out practical guidelines, even borrowed ones, he stayed close to the central theological principles of his hermeneutic, and did not involve himself in laying down narrow rules that would in fact hamper the exegete. Niggling attention to detail in a work like *Christian Doctrine* would only have fostered literal-mindedness and made mockery of what Augustine was trying to do. Only a deep grasp of first principles will suffice as a guide in individual cases, for the interpretation of scripture in the absence of such a grasp of fundamentals is not only imperfect but actually evil.

He is a little more specific when it comes to suggesting how to proclaim the meanings the exegete discovers in scripture. Book 4 of *Christian Doctrine* is a manual of Christian rhetoric for the beginning preacher.[18] No modern reader will intuitively appreciate the break this book made with the past—with late antiquity's past and with Augustine's personal past.

By the late centuries of the Roman empire, ancient education had become almost exclusively education in rhetoric. Lip service was paid to the *artes liberales,* but education was essentially a matter of mastering language. In principle this is no very bad system of general education, but no educational system works very well for very long. The unluckiest systems are the ones that work reasonably well at the outset and, when they begin to falter, are fossilized by an educational public that believes that if one can somehow just get back to doing things the way they were done in the halcyon days, all will be well. This fate had overtaken Roman education.

In the Roman republic, there was a need for the rhetorical education. Young men of the upper classes needed to be skilled orators to succeed in the rough and tumble of public life. By the time the early emperors had made their grip on Roman society unshakeable, rhetoric was useful mainly as a device for flattering the tyrant—still a socially useful skill, but less satisfying to the questioning mind. As time passed, rhetoric became routine, the canon of authors thoroughly studied dwindled to a few classics, and the classroom became ever more remote from the real world. We have only to read Augustine's pagan contemporaries to see how lifeless, stilted, and dull the Latin language could become in some people with the very best late Roman educations.

Augustine himself had been party to this conspiracy of tedium in his early life. For him of all people to write this last book of *Christian Doctrine* was dramatic evidence of the distance he had traveled since abandoning his career as a professor. Where Roman education had become hidebound by rules and pedantry, Augustine here sends a gust of dry, cool wind through the musty cubbyholes of the rhetoricians.

His central heresy, from an ancient point of view, was his insistence that communication is more important than elegance. To be intelligible is a greater thing than to be stylish. "What is the use of a perfect speech," he asks, "that the audience cannot follow, when there is no reason for speaking at all if the people we are talking to do not understand us?" (4.10.24). We hear the preacher rather than the teacher, a man who now had a message of pressing urgency to get across and was willing to consider seriously what was needed to make his point. This was what late Roman education had been missing: something to say. He advocated a "diligent negligence," conscious of the paradox, indeed exploiting its fruitfulness. (Though capable of the high style—as in Book 1 of *City of God*—Augustine as preacher preferred a simple, direct style, artful but lucid.) Augustine is short on specifics. He contents himself with naming the three levels of style (the humble, the ordinary, and the elevated), not so much to exhaust the possibilities as to suggest them and to make the point that there was more than one way to preach the Word (4.18–26).[19]

Apart from the simplicity of Augustine's approach and his insistence on clarity over elegance, the role of theology in this rhetoric would have dismayed an ancient rhetorician as well. What is Augustine's last, pressing hint for the beginning preacher? To begin every proclamation with prayer (4.30.63). The preacher of the Word of God must be in touch with God in order to preach well. He should practice what he preaches (4.27.59). Rhetorical skill in antiquity could be developed entirely independent of commitment to the truth or falsehood of what one was saying; knowledge could be detached from life, but not for Augustine.

Hence the justification for the most practical of his suggestions: when in doubt, quote scripture (4.5.8). Extensive quotation is one guarantee, however limited, that God will speak through the preacher and reach the audience. Beyond that, the preacher himself will grow accustomed to thinking of the language of scripture as a system of discourse in which he feels at home. The best preacher is the one at home with the language of God.

Augustine's exegesis, seen now in the completeness of his theory, is wholly self-effacing. Exegesis has no ultimate worth, nor is a career as exegete something to be aspired to in itself. Only if inter-

pretation ends by removing itself from between the reader of the
sacred text and his God is it successful. If it remains, it is as a
barrier rather than an instrument and contributes nothing to the
happiness of either interpreter or audience. The last words of the
book show Augustine proclaiming his diffidence. "I give thanks to
God that I have been able to expound in these four books, with
whatever trivial ability, not what sort of person I myself am—for
I have many failings—but what sort of person he should be who
works at the business of sound instruction—Christian instruction—
not just for his own benefit but for that of others" (4.31.64).

The literary work that probably took Augustine's time and energies immediately after he left *Christian Doctrine* uncompleted was
nothing less than the *Confessions*. From an arid, but theologically
satisfactory, statement of what the Christian interpreter of scripture
(that is to say simply, the Christian) should be, he turned to an
open and honest work of self-revelation that becomes, by its end,
both a work of scriptural interpretation and (almost) an instrument
of divine revelation itself. A connection must exist between the two
works, but we are only beginning to fathom it.

Chapter Three
Christianity and Society
The Critique of Ideology

"Things are seldom what they seem," crooned Little Buttercup, full of a revelation that would transform the society around her. Augustine would have agreed. No a priori reason compels us to think that appearances, depending directly on the subjective experience of the observer, give any very coherent picture of reality. The perceptions that record these appearances have no compelling independent authority. On this point Christianity shares the ground with other philosophical and religious traditions. It holds that there is such a thing as real being, and even that the world of appearances is directly related to the world of real being. But it claims that human perception and reason are for now impotent to deduce the exact nature of that relation, although human beings do not cease to create patterns that claim to define the relation. In short, human beings live in a dream world from which they can be liberated into reality only with help from outside. Hence, revelation.

Revelation is at the center of Augustine's thought, for it functions in the order of knowledge as grace functions in the order of action, and right knowledge and right action are impossible without revelation and grace. Hence at every turn in Augustine we observe that the formal patterns according to which he interprets the world of appearances derive directly from his understanding of the way God's Word works in the world. So *Christian Doctrine* is the necessary preliminary to everything else in Augustine. When we consider his view of what we may somewhat whimsically call "macrotheology," this is especially true. To understand the relationship between Christianity and society is nothing more and nothing less than to open the question of the relation between competing interpretations of the nature of reality. Human societies that evolve without Christianity differ among themselves about the meaning of sense-knowledge and the nature of reality; but Christianity, wherever it appears, makes special claims on the credence of nations. Civil societies form themselves as the visible manifestation of commonly held principles. Taken at this level, Christianity presents a radically different set of ideas about the nature of the world and the way men ought to live within it.[1]

Whether a "Christian society" as such has ever existed or can ever exist is irrelevant. What is important is to understand how the Christian perspective intrudes upon the complacencies of the world-views with which it comes into contact. In Christianity through the centuries there is a constant tension between the actual order of society and the principles Christianity proposes. What Christianity offers is an interpretation of social reality that claims to come completely from outside human society (as revelation) and that sets itself up as an insistent critic of the natural views of fallen men and women. Christianity, as a social organization, is a constant reproach to the secular world and a constant challenge to custom and mores (even when custom itself carries the Christian name).

In theory and in practice, Augustine had words to describe this situation. In theory, his familiar distinction between letter and spirit served him well. The letter represents hard, empirical reality (or at least the world of appearances masquerading as such), things the way they definitely seem to be to the unaided understanding. All of life, without benefit of divine revelation, is a literal narrative, devoid of meaning and value, only an interaction of atoms in the void. But in the presence of revelation, meaning and value take shape under the power of the spirit.

In this way, deep faith and radical nihilism can be located at opposite ends of a spectrum. Between the two lies a whole range of forms of belief and nonbelief. Christianity can take two approaches to those who occupy the middle ground. All vague stirrings of belief can be treated as well-intentioned motion toward God and embraced in the all-enfolding arms of a generous church; or the same failures of total faith can be treated as apostasy from God and consigned to the outer darkness. Paradox again: Christianity takes both positions simultaneously. Christianity must remain, as one recent observer has said, "radically open to all truth and to every value," for the presence of the spirit cannot be denied in any of these stirrings. At the same time, Christianity itself is meaningless unless it gives unyielding witness to the power of grace and total commitment to the truth of revelation. So radical is the Christian claim that the latter position is the one that usually predominates in Christian discourse.

Because Augustine never ceased to challenge the ideologies of the secular world with the Christian message, he insisted on drawing the line between letter and spirit (between, that is, fantasy and reality, between the world-as-appearance and the world-as-reality) as high and as sharp as he could. Even those in this world who see the message of the spirit with rare clarity are still not fully assimilated to the reality the spirit betokens. Only death can free them from "the body of this death" (Rom. 7.24) and bring them home to authentic reality and true being, to God.

Thus even members in good standing of the visible church were still themselves more on the side of the sinners than of the blessed. They are separated from those around them not by any final distinction (that must await Judgment Day) but by the intermediate distinction that is the result of grace working in their lives. The boundary between the saved and the damned in this world, as long as people live, is completely permeable. The church does not seal itself off from the world around it, but remains permanently, vulnerably, open to it. Those outside can still come in at any time—and those inside can fail, and fall, at any time. (This way of putting the Augustinian case leaves aside the difficult subjects of grace, predestination, and perseverance that must be faced when the relation of Christ to the individual soul is taken up. For the moment we can speak in social terms, with no window into individual souls.)

The implications of this view for our attitude toward natural society are simple but staggering: The mass of humanity lives in a fantasy world. Human societies, created by sinful men and women, are all based on mistaken notions of the nature of reality and are merely dream castles. Societies constitute themselves to bring about results that are impossible. Misery, discord, and death are absolute constants in human experience, despite all the advances of civilization. Nevertheless, human beings retain the most touching faith in the power of effort, scientific knowledge, and the innate good will of their fellows to bring about a more rational and just society.

Ordinary men and women, left to their own devices, go on living in their fantasy world. What sets Augustine's Christians apart is a vision of the real nature of the world in which they live, or at least a glimpse of it. This joyful suspicion hardens them to face, and to refuse to take at face value, the world of appearances. The faith and hope of the Christian embolden him to be despairing about civil society. Where it is the natural tendency of human beings to respond to change by clinging to institutions (thereby guaranteeing the destruction of institutions), the Christian can bid farewell to fading institutions and passing loves, secure in a love that lasts forever and a vision of reality that depends for its goodness, not on the fragile creations of fallible mortals, but on the eternal goodness of God.

In Augustine's time, Rome was the center of the world of fantasy. The literature and culture of antiquity presented a society in which a visible civil institution, the Roman empire, embodied all the hopes and expectations of reasonable men. Rome was, everyone knew, eternal. Uncivilized peoples loomed outside the empire but they were no threat to the magnificence of Rome. Vergil's *Aeneid,* read as a paean to imperial Rome, was the center of the literary imagination and the text around which much of this fascination hypnotically revolved.[2] Augustine himself knew that fascination, and in both *City of God* and his *Confessions* he labored long to pay off his debt to Vergil while disentangling himself forever from the mythology of civil power to which Vergil's text lent itself.

Providentially for Augustine, something terrible happened to disturb the civil faith. The sack of Rome by the Visigoths in 410 provided at least the pretext for a reassessment of conventional ideologies. Some people appear to have used the event as an opportunity to attack Christianity for failing to take care of Rome, but Augustine saw that the more lasting message of the event was the weakness of Rome itself. Christianity gave Augustine a perspective from which to view Rome, at least in the imagination, from outside.

So he wrote *City of God,* in terms fit for a non-Christian audience, to provide first Roman history, then all history, with a thoroughgoing Christian interpretation, to show the presence of the spirit in the literal world of appearances. Apologists often use the device Augustine did, writing ostensibly for outsiders, when in reality they speak mainly to insiders whose faith has been shaken (or shown to be insufficient) by events around them. Modern readers do not much appreciate the destructive part of Augustine's argument. To us it takes little effort to believe that the pagan gods of antiquity were not in fact responsible for the rise and greatness of Rome. But in Augustine's own day, his undertaking was still audacious. Plenty of professed Christians were unready to deny that other forms of divine power besides the Christian one had influenced, and could continue to influence, the affairs of men. Even Augustine granted the pagan gods a claim to exist, but saw them only as feeble demons, allowed a small sphere of mischief by an infinitely more powerful deity.

Cleaning house, as Augustine set out to do, of all the lingering faith in divinities other than the Christian one was thus a drastic step to take. The question at issue was, where was reality to be found? Were there many spiritual principles animating material reality and giving it life and meaning, or was there only one? A plurality of experience destroys community. Every man can have his own god and his own pattern. Reality becomes the least common denominator of a plethora of subjective imaginings. For Christianity, on the other hand, reality is the authentic pattern from which the human imagination has defected. The unique, omnipotent God manifests himself throughout history, at all places and at all times, as creator and lord of the world. On this rests the Christian claim to know objective reality.

We now stand at sufficient distance to see how faith in Rome and its greatness had become, by Augustine's time, a crutch on which a distraught and insecure people wanted desperately to be able to lean. The elite of the empire went on deceiving themselves as long as they could, long after the barbarians had come and gone. What Augustine offered was a chance to throw away the crutch.

Scholarship has documented nothing about the late Roman empire more clearly, I would venture, than that it deserved to fall. It had become a military dictatorship, existing to protect and perpetuate itself, regardless of the cost it demanded from its subjects. Augustine's contemporary Salvian, the priest of Marseilles, claimed (with some justification) that barbarian invaders in the western half of the empire were often greeted with open arms as liberators from the oppression of Roman taxation and bureaucracy. Its culture was politically and morally bankrupt. The "successful" half of the empire, the Byzantine east, was better than the west in preserving itself, and lingered through a sterile middle age until final destruction came at the hands of the Turks in 1453. Nothing has come of Byzantium since.

Faced with Rome and the possibility of pluralism, Augustine in the first five books of *City of God* set out to defend the Christian claim of unity. A single divine power, God the father, is the source of all the world of appearances, is the center of the world of the spirit, and is the foundation of all being and goodness. A claim such as this authorizes a human society; for if there is a single source of meaning and value in the world, there can then be agreement on moral principles. Only agreement on moral principles can make a society function. The argument runs through *City of God* (begun at 2.21–24 and taken up again at 19.21) as a debate with ideas from Cicero's *Republic* (a work known to us only in fragments). Moral discord is the sure sign of impending disintegration. To a chaotic society, the Christian church provides a radical life-giving principle that can dwell in the world—for the church is a temporal institution in the service of a higher moral principle.

The first books of *City of God* require more annotation and historical comment than do the later books. The first three books were written with that audience we described above in mind—the refugees from Rome who were haunting the salons of Carthage in the early 410s, lamenting their dismal fate and blaming the Christian God. Those books were published together by the end of 413; the rest of *City of God* becomes more and more general in its appeal and less tied to the immediate polemical situation. The first book is the most closely tied to circumstances. For example, at least a few religious women seem to have been in Africa who had escaped from Rome after suffering outrages at barbarian hands; the largest section of the first book both encourages these women and rebukes those who insulted them. (1.17–27)

The opening books of *City of God,* therefore, demonstrate by negative argument, with polemical verve, that in the order of knowledge, God—the Christian God—prevails alone. What remains is for Augustine to show that this God prevails in the order of action— and love—as well. That is the business of Books 6 through 10.

To show the adequacy of the Christian claims, Augustine confronted the surviving ancient philosophical tradition in debate. He began by making bold admissions. By Augustine's time, the diversity of conflicting philosophical schools (Stoics, Epicureans, Cynics, Academics, etc.) had virtually disappeared. To be a philosopher in the serious sense of that word meant to be a disciple, at some distance, of Plato. Modern writers call this movement Neoplatonism and confer the leadership of the school on Plotinus (d. c. A.D. 265). This is a useful but somewhat imprecise form of reference. The people who belonged to the school called themselves simply Pla-

CITY OF GOD

City of God is a large and complex work. This chart offers the briefest possible sketch of its organization and contents. For fuller discussion, see J.-C. Guy, *Unité et structure logique de la 'Cité de Dieu' de saint Augustin* (Paris, 1961), who takes a different view on some points from that suggested by this chart.

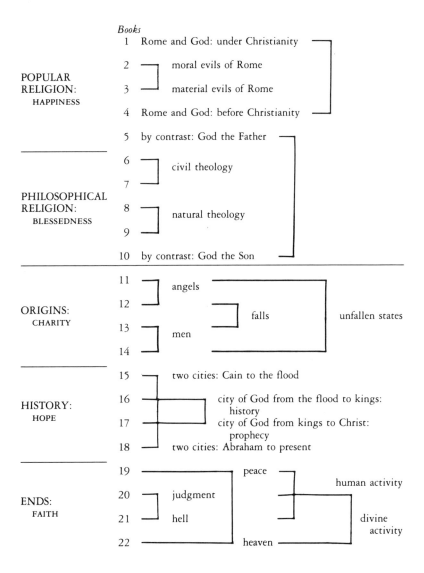

Books

1 Rome and God: under Christianity

POPULAR RELIGION: HAPPINESS

2 moral evils of Rome
3 material evils of Rome
4 Rome and God: before Christianity

5 by contrast: God the Father

PHILOSOPHICAL RELIGION: BLESSEDNESS

6 civil theology
7
8 natural theology
9
10 by contrast: God the Son

ORIGINS: CHARITY

11 angels
12
13 men
14

falls — unfallen states

HISTORY: HOPE

15 two cities: Cain to the flood
16 city of God from the flood to kings: history
17 city of God from kings to Christ: prophecy
18 two cities: Abraham to present

ENDS: FAITH

19 peace
20 judgment
21 hell
22 heaven

human activity — divine activity

tonists and claimed to owe allegiance only to Plato himself, whom
they interpreted in a variety of ways.[3]

What any reader of the surviving works of the Neoplatonists
discovers is that in the realm of speculation, they had much super-
ficially in common with the Christians. In the three *hypostases* of
Plotinian thought one finds a parallel for the three persons of the
Christian trinity; this late Platonism contained a firm belief in the
existence of a single realm of the spirit that gave value and meaning
to the lives of people living in the material world. It softened this
virtual monotheism by allowing that the ancient religions were, in
their various styles, talking about the same thing. The divine spirit
leaked through into the world of matter in a variety of forms,
variously interpreted by ignorant men in a profusion of different
cults. A proper philosophical understanding, the Platonists argued,
would lead to an understanding of the unity of experience.

Augustine introduced the Platonists in *City of God* (see 8.2–12)
so as to deal with the question whether there was any possibility of
salvation without revelation—whether, in short, men's unaided efforts could lead them to right knowledge and hence to virtuous life.
He admitted that the Platonists were great philosophers and wise
men, and acknowledged their virtues, but then he proceeded to
offer an explanation of how this situation had come about in a way
that left the primacy of the Christian interpretation unshaken.

Augustine's argument always had a scriptural basis. In the first
chapter of Romans, Paul sought to justify God's dealings with the
heathens who had not heard God's revelation to the Jews. The
pagans, Paul argued, had no excuse for ignorance. "For the invisible
things of God are clearly known from the [visible] things of creation"
(Rom. 1.20). Thus on the one hand, even in a fallen world, direct,
unaided knowledge of God remained possible, in the sense that
those who failed to achieve it were blameworthy for their failure,
but impossible, in the sense that in this fallen world no one ever
achieves direct knowledge of God.

To remedy this defect of human reason, revelation was given to
mankind through the instrument of the church. In practice for
Augustine it is only through the revelation of the spirit in the
church that true knowledge can be acquired. What then of the
Platonists? They are allowed by God to exist to offer corroborating
evidence. As the most excellent and reputable of philosophical schools
of antiquity, they are seen to have gone a long way toward under-

standing the basic truths of theology (as seen by Christians), without ever getting the whole picture. Formally, then, Augustine's argument in Books 6 through 10 of *City of God* is this: If the best of philosophers (best by virtue of the nearness of their approximation to Christian theology, as well as by virtue of their reputation among men), cannot achieve a complete and adequate picture of the divine dispensation for salvation, a fortiori no other philosophical sect can provide such a picture. Without such accurate knowledge, salvation is impossible.

Philosophy fails in another, somewhat more significant way as well. It has no place to stand. Philosophical knowledge takes the form of individual comments about the nature of things emitted by learned and serious men on no authority except their own. Philosophers may think that their conclusions are self-evident and may chafe at the unbelief of the masses in the face of their sober and well-reasoned arguments. But Augustine saw that this is not only a likely result, but a necessary one, in a fallen world.

One thing that was lost in the fall of man was the trust that underlies all human communication. The story of the tower of Babel (Gen. 11. 1–9) implied that sin renders every individual an isolated fragment of consciousness, cut off from the consolation of shared experience. If civil societies are created by men as fraudulent attempts to duplicate the unity they instinctively desire but cannot achieve, so too in the philosophical order, when the most pressing issues of salvation and happiness are at stake, the most men can do is create new sects and philosophies, small attempts at an intellectual tour-de-force by which a few individuals will pretend to have transcended the conditions of human ignorance to attain real knowledge.

But such constructions in the realm of the spirit are no less fraudulent than great empires in the realm of matter. Philosophical schools come and go, and the mass of mankind is left alone, with no profit to show for all its deference to the sages. Philosophy, finally, is so individualistic that it becomes undemocratic. Only the initiated few can achieve the heroic feats of knowledge and thought that make them philosophers. Their less learned fellows are condemned to make do with the much less satisfactory frauds perpetrated by the pagan religions. Augustine, speaking for Christianity, insists that if there is any salvation at all in this world, it must be accessible to all, not merely to those with the money and leisure to pursue university studies in philosophy.

In place of the sages then, Christianity offered a mediator, adequate and unique, not only between what was divine and what was human, but even between human beings themselves. Where the philosophers had only the arid consolations of logic, Augustine preached the power of Christ. In Christ the divine principle entered the world, revealing the will of God and providing a common basis for the mutual understanding (and love) of all those who accepted him. Christian theology challenges the self-centered intellectual autonomy of the philosophers by insisting on self-surrender and acceptance of a power of knowledge coming, not from effort and innate virtue, but from outside the individual.

The central paradox of Christianity underlies its doctrine. On one hand, mankind is utterly responsible for its actions and its failures to achieve salvation independently—hence the justice of damnation; but on the other hand, God intervenes in the affairs of fallen mankind to provide a certain and independent means of redemption—hence the mercy of salvation. For Augustine's contemporaries, this ineffable combination of justice and mercy could be the largest stumbling block to Christianity.

But for now, while he was writing *City of God,* the logical ramifications of this theory were not yet his concern. The purpose of the first ten books of *City of God* was demolition, not construction. Much of his rhetorical skill went into making the Christian alternative to the pagan claims emerge almost effortlessly and inevitably once the pagan arguments were disposed of. The first five books cleared the central position for God the father and creator in the disposition of the affairs of the material world, while the next five books blast away at the pagan interpretation of the ordering of affairs in the world of understanding and the spirit. When the smoke clears, God the son, Christ the redeemer, appears at the center of the picture, the true power for salvation of individual souls.

Where the first five books required historical annotation and illustration, the second five require what is in some ways a more difficult effort of understanding. Augustine shared with his opponents a common view of the reality of what we would call supernatural phenomena. He did not need to debunk all claims of miraculous intervention into nature by spirits other than the Christian God; he could simply revalue them as works of the demons, the fallen angels of whom scripture spoke. All this makes alien reading for us, but we should envy Augustine the polemical situation in which he found himself. He merely had to explain the mysterious supernatural events his opponents alleged; the skeptic is in the far more difficult position of having to deny the supernatural features of the events outright.

Whether we should give credence to the ancient tendency to see miracles everywhere is another question, not addressed by *City of God*. Augustine himself was for many years disinclined to accept the probability of Christian miracle in his own day (holding that it had been a special gift to the generation of the apostles), but later shifted his position and in the last book of *City of God* a whole dossier of contemporary miracle stories (almost entirely limited to cures of the sick) may be found (22.8). Augustine did not possess anything like the same conception of natural/supernatural that we bring to such stories; what was important for early Christians in miracle stories was not the event itself (which was merely one more surprise in a surprising world), but the meaning of the event. The New Testament speaks of miracles by Greek words that mean "signs and portents," and even the word "miracle" itself derives from a Latin word meaning "marvelous." In both languages the ancient focus was on the reaction of the observer, drawing from the event meaning for his own life. The deity manipulated human affairs in such a way as to bring about this communication. Seen objectively, the theology of miracle had something of the qualities of a self-fulfilling prophecy. If a miracle was something that was meant to astonish and communicate a theological message (whatever the nature of the event itself), then all the miracles recorded by the early church were truly miraculous.

Thus Augustine could readily exploit the credulity of the pagan world from which Christianity arose to establish the polemical structure of the first ten books of *City of God*. In them he demonstrated the ruling power of God (Books 1 through 5) and the redeeming power of Christ (Books 6 through 10) as the only adequate hypothesis to explain the ways of the world. The world in which the pagans had lived, be it the material world of Rome or the spiritual world of the philosophers and demons, did not exist. It was a kingdom of fraud, built by fallen human minds attempting to make sense of the world around them. Augustine was not insensitive to the nobility and high intentions of the pagan sages, but he could not blind himself either to their failures. At the end of the first ten books of *City of God*, Augustine stood poised between pagan and Christian

worlds, having shown the failure of the pagan world-view and in-
timated the necessity of the Christian. His business in the books
that followed would be to turn away from the world that antiquity
had made and show how Christianity proposed that men and women
go about living in the real, fallen world.

The People of God

Christianity defies time and validates history. On the one hand,
the eternal vision of God is the norm against which human notions
of time are judged and found wanting; sacramental actions destroy
the supremacy of time, while eternal happiness, outside the tunnel
of transience, awaits the blessed. On the other hand, history has
unique value. Christ died once for mankind's sins and need not
repeat the sacrifice. Cyclical theories of history are ruled out and
the whole pattern of human life is given a linear purpose.

Indeed, Christianity may be said to have invented history in the
modern sense of the term. Before Christianity, ancient writers of
what we call history were often little more than sententious purvey-
ors of recent memories and old legends; at best, they chronicled the
events of their own society in light of hindsight and their own
philosophical preoccupations. Each generation lived isolated in time
from all others, with only the traditions and institutions of the
political realm—as the ancient religions faded—to offer escape from
time into history. Christianity introduced the notion that the history
of the world might have a single pattern. A beginning, a middle,
and an end spring up around the whole of human existence. Instead
of an endless succession of solipsisms, there is a single human community, united across time and space, to which the Christian belongs.

This is the vision of the human condition that Augustine unfolds
in the last dozen books of *City of God*. His divisions are simple:
beginning/middle/end, or rather past/present/future. What we would
recognize as history is all in the middle section, devoted to the
world after the fall and before the last judgment, suspended in the
material interim but revolving around the presence of Christ.
The tasks Augustine set for himself in these books were to explain
the fall of man and its implications; then to prescribe the Christian
remedy for the ills of the present; and finally to explain the Christian
hope for the world to come.

First, the fall. Augustine knew full well that the seven days of
creation were a literary figure for a much more complex process

whose temporal duration he did not care to speculate about (11.6–8). Similarly, he believed in the historicity of the story of Adam and Eve, but he did so in a world in which there was literally no reason why he should not believe the story. He would not have found it difficult to adjust his views to accord with the development of modern anthropology. Indeed, the Augustinian theory of original sin becomes much easier to defend when the mythic qualities of the Adam and Eve story are recognized. The result is that, in the terms we discussed concerning *Christian Doctrine,* Augustine cheerfully accepts the literal meaning of the Genesis story, but passes quickly on to what he knows is more important, the spiritual meaning. Until the story's ramifications are applied to the whole church and to each Christian, there is no point in lingering over its details.

"Two loves gave birth to two cities" (14.28). In this statement all the doctrine of *City of God* is summarized, and in it we see reflected the more abstract formulas of *Christian Doctrine.* The selfless love of God ("enjoyment") was replaced in Adam and Eve by love of self, manifest in the first instance as the pride that leads to disobedience.

Augustine always emphasizes the rebelliousness the first sin entailed. The precise command God gave was irrelevant. What mattered was that the serpent appealed to the selfish longings of the first couple, and that appeal found a willing response. Though repentance swiftly followed error, the pattern was instilled in the human race once and for all. For Augustine, the fact of sin in the world around him, the fact that men and women enter the world in a state of separation from God, found corroboration in the biblical story of the first couple. He never found a satisfactory theory to explain the transmission of original sin, but of the fact of its presence he had no doubt at all.[4]

But *City of God* sets the human story of original sin in a wider context. The first error of Adam and Eve was not something innate in them, but the response to a suggestion that came from outside. Hence Augustine goes at great lengths into the origins of the two cities in the fall of the angels. Satan was the highest of creatures, so he fell the lowest. Pride again (the notion that the self is supremely lovable) was the seed of evil. This planted in the world of creation the possibility of evil for man. Humanity seems to be given the second chance offered by Christianity because it was not itself the source of all the evil in creation. The fallen angels enjoy no such redemptive favor.

Thus from the heights of heaven to the depths of hell there are created two separate societies of angels and men, with a boundary between the two societies that runs right through the earthly world. Augustine calls those societies *civitates,* which we usually translate "cities," but which more precisely meant "communities," that is, cities in their human dimension. The reasons for Augustine's choice of this metaphor are deeply rooted in his theological writings. One obvious implication was that it enabled him to pick up again the theme of pilgrimage he had used in *Christian Doctrine* and elsewhere.[5]

The material world, then, is disputed territory, where the enemy holds sway for the moment. The followers of Christ, the citizens of the heavenly city, must live in this world as foreigners (*peregrini,* "pilgrims") do, using the laws of the city in which they find themselves to shelter themselves, but always planning and preparing to leave that city behind to return home. For those of the earthly city, the earth seems (wrongly) to be home and they treat it as such, abandoning their claim to citizenship above.

This theme looms all through these books. First, however, Augustine had to explain fallenness itself and what it entails, for it seemed he had painted himself into a logical corner. God created all things, and insofar as they were created by God, they were good; evil, then, is the mere absence of good, not—as the Manicheans claimed—an independent power in itself. How then came evil into the world?

Not as a material presence, Augustine would say. Natural disasters may trouble the hearts of men, but they are not truly evil. Evil resides only in the rational souls of fallen angels and men. Those souls are, for Augustine, tripartite: the human soul exists, knows, and loves.[6] The moral worth of the individual lies in the quality of the love, that is to say, the quality of the will, and evil results from a turning of the will's love away from the things it should seek (enjoyment of God, love of neighbor) to other things (usually self-love).

So how does the will, created good by a good God, turn to evil? Augustine does not know, nor can anyone know. "Seek not to find the efficient cause of an evil will. It is not a matter of efficiency, but of deficiency. . . . To defect from the one who is the highest being to something that has less being, this is to begin to have an evil will. To seek the causes of such a defect—deficient causes, not efficient ones—is like trying to see darkness or to hear silence" (12.7). Evil is a nothing, and a turning to evil has no cause (all causation is divinely ordered and hence good) but is entirely self-generated. The most that can be said is that God created rational creatures with wills genuinely free so their worship of God would be a source of glory. The source of evil is, finally, a mystery, and a mystery that all of Augustine's later debates with the Pelagians never tempted him to pretend he had solved.

More than logical trickery underlies this evasive answer. If the turning of the soul towards evil were rational and comprehensible, there would be something good about it, since all reason is good. Everything in the world that is intelligible is intelligible by virtue of its reflection of God's creative power. When the will turns away from God it thus separates itself from the goodness of creation into a self-created darkness that is no longer intelligible. The real question was not so much how evil arose, but what it meant. The condition of fallen men and women preoccupies Augustine through Books 11–14. He concludes that the fall from grace led as well to a kind of fall from freedom. Human beings after the fall remained entirely responsible for their moral failings, which come about only as a result of their own free acts (on the hypothesis that original sin is justifiably imputed to each individual at birth). But fallen people are not, because of the chains forged by sin, capable of restoring themselves to God's favor by their own efforts. By choosing to assert their own power rather than submit to God's, they discover how powerless they are.

The most palpable manifestation of fallen human nature is concupiscence, the importunate nagging of the flesh's desires. In the fall, the natural order and harmony of the person were thrown into confusion. The will turned from God, knowledge was darkened with ignorance, and a debilitating derangement of the will resulted. Thus, the higher faculties of the person were no longer in control as they were when the natural hierarchy of the soul was undisturbed. The ensuing disorder is most visible in the appetites of the flesh.

Augustine began with the observation of a pastor that it is in human sexuality that the confusion and disorder of sin are most visible. Treating sexuality as a biological question, he observed that human beings are scarcely masters of their own bodies, unable to subject the sexual organs to rational control. Treating sexuality as a psychological question, he saw the same recurring failure of control and discipline. From Paul he heard confirmation of what he saw: "I see another law in my members, warring against the law of my mind, and bringing me into captivity to the law of sin" (Rom. 7.23). The history of human relations is full of good intentions overthrown by powerful appetites, a plight that cannot be blamed only on repressive social conventions.

But sexuality remained for Augustine fundamentally, even supernaturally good. His (in many ways comical) depiction of what sex would have been like in the Garden of Eden if Adam and Eve had not fallen shows him earnestly (and perhaps even with conscious whimsy) attempting to give concrete form to his recognition of the fundamental values of sexuality (14.21–27). To what extent Augustine may be made the parent of later attitudes toward sexuality that now seem unduly negative is open to doubt; he did hold that virginity was superior to marriage, but emphasized repeatedly that both states of life were inherently good; he held that the purpose of sexual intercourse was procreation and that even in marriage it was otherwise culpable, but he was careful to minimize the burden of that fault. His contemporary Jerome had engaged in a famous battle of pamphlets with Jovinian, a monk who held views of sexuality that sound refreshingly modern; Jerome is far more negative than Augustine.[7]

But the implications of fallenness run far beyond the disorder of human sexuality. In sexuality, lack of control manifests itself at every level of society. But that lack of control stemming from confusion and selfishness is characteristic of human affairs of all sorts in all times and places. The disorder began with the fall of the angels and entered history with the fall of Adam. Indeed, it may be said that "history" in the limited sense we now use is the result of the conjunction of human beings with sin. The middle four books of the last part of *City of God,* Books 15–18, recount the present condition of human society, between the first sin and the last judgment, while the two societies (heavenly and earthly) find themselves mingled together and doing battle with each other in the arena of human society.

Such is the world of fallen man: the good mixed with the bad, seemingly inextricable: "These two cities are intertwined here in this world and entangled with each other, until they are to be separated at the last judgment" (1.35). No vision here of the saintly few penned up temporarily among the mass of the damned, waiting for release; rather, the boundary between the two societies runs through the hearts of individual men and women. The two societies cannot be identified and distinguished in this world: that is an absolute condition of fallenness.

Powerful forces in Augustine's time sought to identify the heavenly society with one visible institution, with the Christian empire itself. Greek Christians in particular had concluded that even biblical prophecy spoke of the coming age of happiness under Christian emperors. They assumed that a special grace could be seen in the Roman empire that had now given itself over to Christ.[8] This attitude grew and developed in the Middle Ages, producing abundant imperial and papal misconceptions. Augustine himself was invoked as a patron of this ideology, in a way that merits notice.

Augustine opposed all such identification of earthly societies with the heavenly society of which the church is an earthly shadow. Even when he engaged in panegyric of a recent emperor,[9] he saw virtue in such an emperor only when he found personal submission to the church of Christ. But Augustine made one crucial mistake in judgment that led to much confusion later. In the early 410s, a young priest from Spain named Orosius came to Africa seeking Augustine's advice on theological controversies in his homeland. While he was there, Augustine apparently delegated him (we have only Orosius's word on this) to compile a history of the calamities of the human race, to show pagans that the Christian reading of history was true. (In Book 3 of *City of God* Augustine declined to outline his position in detail, fearing to become a "mere writer of history" [3.18].) Orosius, however, did not fully grasp Augustine's ideas, but his energy quickly produced seven books of universal history destined to have a wide readership in the Middle Ages.[10] Augustine never actually disowned Orosius, but it is clear from Books 15–18 of *City of God* that Orosius had gone astray. Orosius wrote as though church, empire, and heavenly city could be identified in one confused mishmash. The medieval audience was often readier to read Orosius's exciting (and gory) narrative than to plod through twenty-two books of *City of God,* thinking to find Augustine's doctrine in Orosius's pages. Given the extent of the medieval misrepresentation of Augustine that ensued,[11] it is worth examining his attitude toward earthly societies (including "Christian empires") in some detail. The first principle is paramount: that earthly societies contain, just as people do, an undistinguishable mixture of good and evil.

Only if that point is kept in mind can the redemptive power of Christ in Augustinian thought be fully appreciated. First, the coming of Christ gives sense to history. It places a fixed and final benchmark by which all other events are measured. But the heavenly city had been represented on earth before Christ's coming as well as after. Cain and Abel were the earthly founders of both cities, and throughout the Old Testament Augustine traces the pre-Christian history of redemption. The Old Testament patriarchs did not merit salvation by their own deeds, for the grace that saved them was the grace Christ brought. Though Christ came at a particular time, his grace pervades history.

Christianity and the church hold a central, but temporary place in the drama of salvation history. They embrace the imperfection of human existence in the fallen world, and like this world they will pass away. What is genuinely important for all men is the ultimate progress toward union with God. Those who are outwardly in God's good favor (as loyal members of the Christian church) but who are finally found wanting in divine judgment have never been part of the heavenly city, appearances notwithstanding. Similarly, those who have not been visible members of the church but who do experience the transforming reality of God's grace (in Augustine's explicit discussion these people are limited to the Old Testament figures, but nothing he says compels us to keep the limits there) win final union with God.

In all this drama, Christianity and the church are far from irrelevant. The paradox is that they are essential and yet dispensable. The message of grace could not have come into the world without them, and the church continues to bear the special marks of divine favor that make it a sure guide and a channel of grace. More than that, it is pointless to speculate. Faith and hope, not assurance, are the marks of a Christian believer.

So, paradoxically, history is entirely changed by the intervention of Christ—and nothing is changed. To the world of appearance, only appearances change. A new religion comes to compete with the others, a new clique of the self-proclaimed elect declares itself. But in reality, divine grace works unceasingly in the hidden recesses of the lives of all those who open themselves to it. Much mystery surrounds the encounter of grace and the will, and that mystery characterizes the church in the world. But for Augustine in *City of God,* the elucidation of the ambiguity is less important than the recognition of its main features.

Augustine's historical vision is far from narrow. The actions of Christ and his church have affected only a portion of the human race in the conventional view of history, but for Augustine it is the Christian revelation that gives all history its meaning. All history is salvation history. The meaning given to human life by Christ by a single intervention is true for all men and women everywhere. The message is sent forth to all nations, and all nations can be called to receive it. This is the finality of the Christian message. What remains is to be revealed, in the last days, will be revealed in accord with what is already known, and no less universally. Despite its recursions into various forms of exclusivity, Christianity gave the world the first vision of human history as a coherent and organized whole, not merely as a welter of mutually hostile exclusivities.

For Augustine's account of human history in Books 15–18, the primary text is always scripture. This may appear to imply a kind of exclusivity in itself until we recall that according to the principles laid down in *Christian Doctrine,* the allegorical interpretation of that scripture is the medium by which the apparent exclusivity of the text is broken down and the pertinence of every page to every age of history is clarified. Thus, when Augustine expounds the spiritual, or allegorical, sense of scripture, he uses the limited text of scripture as a key to unlock a vision wider than the text.

In this comprehensive view of human history, so trivial and evanescent a thing as the Roman empire plays little part. Augustine had no wish to deny the achievements of that empire, for in the world Augustine knew the Roman empire was easily the most extensive and the longest-lasting exercise ever undertaken in creating a substitute for paradise. But the Augustine who had once proclaimed an emperor's praises could, with the guidance of the Christian message, tear himself away from the secular vision of Roman glory. Once he did so, it was easy to turn back to the Roman world and see it as no more ultimately meaningful than a modern scholar would.

By the time Augustine came to the end of Book 18, he was ready to recapitulate the results of his attempt to disentangle human affections from human creations. Book 19 contains his vision of human society seen *sub specie aeternitatis.*[12] The evocation of peace, true peace, the goal of human life even in fraudulent human societies created by sinful people is profoundly appealing.

The subject is approached in several ways. A long and whimsically pedantic analysis traces the 288 possible philosophical approaches to happiness that the Roman polymath Varro had outlined (19.1– 4). All are reduced to one way, the Christian way. An old quarrel with Cicero, postponed from Book 2, is taken up to show that where justice is absent true community cannot exist (19.21). In communities robbed of justice by original sin, the real peace of an ideal society cannot exist. (He had earlier asked, "What are kingdoms without justice? Mere bands of hoodlums" [4.4].)

The Christian community lives on, loving the true peace of the heavenly Jerusalem, devoid of illusions about the transient world in which it finds itself. This illusionless existence gives the Christian church a detachment from the secular world that in practice it does not always maintain. While secular governments attempt to create lasting peace in a world destined to know only strife and struggle until the last days, there is a subversive quality about the life that Augustine imagines for the church in these circumstances. She is, he says, to "use the peace of Babylon" (19.26), that is to say, to take advantage of all the limited and partial peace that human society can find for itself, without ever settling for that peace. She is to use, not enjoy, the peace of the earthly city, and always to keep her eyes focused on the ultimate goal. As citizens of the heavenly city, Christians are always to recall where their true allegiance lies.

What then of the warfare of the earthly city? Augustine is often invoked as a kind of patron saint of the Just War. The passage in City of God in which he expounds his theory in its greatest detail deserves quotation in full: "But the wise man, they say, will wage just wars. Surely, if he remembers that he is a human being, he will much rather lament the need to wage even just wars. For if they were not just he would not have to fight them and there would be no wars for him. The injustice of the opposing side is what imposes the duty of waging wars" (19.7). For Augustine, the Christian's job is to resist, conceding the justice of a cause only with reluctance, always on the lookout for the moment justice deserts his own cause. The siege of his own Hippo in the last months of his life seemed to Augustine a conflict both just and wretched, a calamity for the people he had served lovingly for forty years.[13]

In earthly terms, the vision of human society *City of God* provides is unremittingly bleak, even if indisputable. Most human societies, enamored with the daydreams of politics, pretend the human condition is better than it is. Men forget history because they do not want to remember that others have gone down paths of prosperity and complacency before them. But in western Christianity since Augustine there has always been a prophetic voice to proclaim the ultimate weakness of human political societies. Christianity offers mankind a hope beside which the gloom of the human condition is as nothing. Christian theology after Augustine is always hopeful and, in the deepest sense, optimistic. But for those who reject that theology, the vision of human society that is left is stark and terrifying. In this sense as well, all history is salvation history. The salvific quality of that history makes it possible to be realistically honest about the damnable qualities of life in the interim; there are no easy ways out for Augustine.

In the last three books of *City of God,* Augustine gives substance to his hope. At the close of human history in the present age, there come the last things: death, judgment, heaven, and hell. Eschatological thought animated the early church long after it became clear that the second coming would not occur in the lifetime of the apostles. The fathers are not being morbid and gloomy when they speak of last things at times of material and moral crisis in their society; eschatology is hope. We have lived too long in a society growing from Christian roots and we are too familiar with the most vivid and negative representations of eschatological themes to be able to see that hope fresh when we encounter those themes in the ancient writers.

Augustine is in fact as restrained as a modern liberal theologian in his depiction of what lies ahead. He knew the alluring dangers of too-explicit representations for popular piety and contented himself instead with insisting on the most abstract of outlines of future life. At one place he does list the principal scriptural manifestations that are prophesied to accompany the last days, but he promptly qualifies what he says by adding that he is sure all these things will happen, but he cannot be certain of the order in which they will occur, nor does he think that the list is in any way exhaustive (20.30). He feels deeply the deceptive quality of metaphor in such description. Human language is always a broken instrument, and thus it labors under a double burden. Not only is the language itself suspect, but it draws its terms of reference entirely from a world that is suspect as well. The notion of life itself is only partial and inadequate in human experience and language. Whatever it is that the blessed will experience in their union with God—that is life, and what we now experience is metaphor, even though language tries to make it the other way around.

Augustine's discussion of the afterlife thus does not establish a clear picture of what awaits, but instills expectant hope, while nurturing the faith and trust that will enable the hopeful to accept what they find. The weakness of the human mind and its language is just too great in the face of the greatest of mysteries. Theology can only instill reverence and leave behind a residue of hope.

So far the purposes and so far the plan of *City of God*. Ten books outline the weaknesses of the secular vision of history embodied in Roman life and thought, then twelve books sketch the pattern of history, putting life here below in the middle panel of a triptych, with God the creator standing before and God the judge standing after. This vision of history draws authority entirely from outside the conventional limits of history, and hence can claim for the transient affairs of time-bound men and women a dimension of meaning no secular ideology can manage. We will debate to the end of time whether any vision such as Augustine's can be valid or not. Augustine himself would expect this, since the final revelation is by definition withheld until precisely the end of time. For the time being (which is, Augustine would point out, all we have) the rhetorical and polemical power of Augustine's vision in undermining the claims of Rome and supplanting them with the claims of his own community was dramatic.

Chapter Four
Christ and the Soul

The lofty theology of a book like *City of God* is always a little irrelevant. All of it may be true. A full understanding of the dispensation of salvation may be impossible without it. But in the end it is just another construction of the human intellect. Even if the intellect is aided by divine illumination, its triumphs are still fleeting ones.

How God deals with the human race may be a matter of speculative interest. How Christ redeems the individual soul is an urgent concern. The individual person has no other life but his own. The Christian who believes in his God and longs to be united with him deems all other concerns secondary, however important. The abuse this zeal fosters is selfish concentration on personal salvation at the expense of a caring involvement in human affairs, but to Augustine such concentration is always self-defeating. The path to personal salvation lies through a future of personal self-abnegation in the love of God and of neighbor. Paradoxically, to save one's soul means abandoning all morbid preoccupation with self by immersion in self-effacing love. "He who would save his soul must lose it" (Matthew 10.39). Thus, it is "microtheology" that presents Augustine's vision of Christianity in its fullest development and that attracted the fiercest controversy. In the last two decades of Augustine's life, the Pelagian controversy forced him to examine his views on these subjects with passionate care. What emerged in that period was a fuller statement of principle and a working out of logical consequences, but not a new theology.[1]

The rudiments of the Augustinian theology of grace can be seen as early as the first book of the *Seven Various Questions for Simplicianus,* written in the mid-390s when Augustine confronted the paradoxes of Paul's letter to the Romans. Augustine was fortunate, however, to be able to pursue his argument with the Pelagians in logical sequence, which we will attempt to duplicate here. The central concerns are threefold: sin (the condition of mankind left to itself), grace (the act of redemption in Christ), and predestination (the condition of the liberated soul—the most mysterious matter of all, and most fraught with complexities arising from the effect of grace on the will).

The first thing Augustine wrote against the ideas of Pelagius (of whom he had barely heard himself) was *The Guilt and Remission of Sin; and Infant Baptism,* written in 411 in response to questions from his friend Marcellinus.[2] In this pamphlet he dealt with the fact, as he saw it, of original sin and raised the further questions about grace to be answered in *Spirit and Letter,* to which we shall turn shortly. Fifteen more years of controversy were to elapse before his final views on predestination and free will were set down in the work that will occupy us last, *The Predestination of the Blessed* (429).

Sin

The human animal is a moral animal, and its plight is dismal. The best of intentions demonstrably lead to the most disastrous of conclusions, and even the best of intentions are but rarely sovereign. Human beings have an irrepressible capacity for disappointing themselves and each other with their thoughts, words, and deeds. Conscience is more than a chain by which the human mind irrationally constrains itself, and is at least the evidence of a tension and dissatisfaction deeply planted in the race. The material world presents us with things as they are (or seem to be) and does so brutally. But in the realm of the mind, we consider things as they should be. The origins of the moral instincts may be baffling, but their tenacity in the face of all discouragement is great. No vision of human nature is adequate without an explanation of the nature of moral evil.

In Christian theology, the explanation is simple and blunt. The human race is separated, temporarily but drastically, from the consoling source of being and goodness. Alone in a world from which they have tried to banish God, men act as irresponsible children suddenly lacking clear guidance and immediate punishment. As we saw in the last chapter, the history of the species is the story of the separation and reunification of creatures and creator. In the pages of revelation the separation is documented by the example of Adam. In *City of God* Augustine saw in the fall of Adam an essential mystery: Evil enters the world, it persists, but it consists of nothing more than the perversity of dependent creatures, fleetingly anonymous in their rebellion. Through sin, death and all misery entered the world. The wounds of life are all self-inflicted.

But what does the sin of the first parents have to do with the present misery? The weakest link in Augustine's theology of sin is his view on the transmission of original sin. Literal acceptance of the Adam and Eve story created difficulties for him that he need not have faced. Throughout his life he visibly inclined to a theory of physical propagation, according to which the disorder of the sexual appetites discussed above was not only the sign of sin but the instrument of its transmission—hence, perhaps, a special suspicion of sexuality. But it is also indisputable that Augustine was aware of the dangers of this theory and ultimately refused to commit himself to any particular hypothesis on the origins of individual human souls and the transmission of Adam's sin. Instead, he confined himself to what he was sure of, namely the sin of Adam and the presence of his sin in the species. Given those two points, the mechanism of transmission was of less than supreme importance, and Augustine could indulge in an agnosticism that maddened some of his contemporaries (and almost all of posterity).

In summary, he concludes that original sin is innate in human beings, even though the responsibility for that sin does, quite fairly, inhere in each individual. The paradox here is clear: original sin comes from Adam, but is the responsibility of each individual. Here again, the pragmatic approach satisfied Augustine. To those who would debate the fairness of this system of transmission, he would simply point out that every individual, from the earliest age, is in fact a sinner. From even before the access of knowledge and reason (the conditions we are accustomed to associate with moral responsibility) there is the clear presense of selfishness—the basis of evil—and willed disobedience.[3]

And yet original sin differs from actual sin, that is, sin committed by the individual. The sinfulness of the individual infant is not itself the same thing as original sin, but only the evidence of the sinful propensities that original sin generates. Original sin brings with it all the penalties discussed in *City of God,* and even when the responsibility for original sin is taken away, the purely temporal damage (that is, the harm done to the species in the material world) remains. Actual sin, on the other hand, does much less harm by its secondary, temporal ill effects (sometimes none at all, at least to the naked eye), while carrying with it a higher degree of responsibility and potentially eternal damage for the soul of the sinner.

Original sin is sufficient to deny the individual eternal blessedness, but only actual sin can win real damnation.

Sin is not then a matter of chance or choice. Original sin is present in all from the outset and is the reason for the continued propensity to sin that afflicts the species. Men do not begin tabula rasa, blissful in ignorance and poised in sublime neutrality somewhere between good and evil (a preposterous position, given Augustine's definitions of good and evil), able to earn praise for doing good and blame for doing evil. Instead, all men and women start with a handicap. Even when the eternal consequences of original sin are removed by baptism, it still affects the soul so that every human being eventually succumbs to sin.

This doctrine is fundamental to Augustine. It contributes to his skepticism about the intellectual powers of mankind and hence to his reliance on divine revelation. It also made him see the history of the species as a struggle with sin brought to an end only when divine goodness intervenes and liberates men for eternity. But theory and practice are never far apart in Augustine, and there are practical, pastoral considerations as well.

From earliest times, Christianity had preached baptism in Christ, a baptism of the spirit. Liturgically, baptism had been part of Christian worship from the time of the apostles. Theologically, it came to be understood as the act by which the church, transmitting the power of the spirit in the world, welcomed sinners into its midst with a free gift of forgiveness from the burden of sin. The power of forgiveness in the church had then to be deployed in a different way to cope with the persistent sinfulness of the baptised Christian. In Augustine's own time penance was still public; private confession is a medieval innovation in the main. The cumbersome and frightening penitential discipline (whose validity was periodically challenged by such as the Novatians and Donatists) had conspired to encourage many, like the emperor Constantine, to postpone baptism—the one sovereign remedy for sin—until the deathbed. Pastorally, this solution was unacceptable, since it seemed to provide carte blanche for sin through the whole of life, so long as sacramental grace was accessible at the very end. (That accessibility had a disturbing correlation to the wealth and social position of the sinner; pagan criticism of Christianity made much of this aspect of church practice.)

By Augustine's day, timely baptism was becoming more the rule. But when did the need for baptism emerge? Was it only a remedy for the sin of the conscious, reasoning individual? Or did it speak to the underlying sinfulness innate in the species? Given the views Augustine cherished, it is not surprising that he chose the latter answer, and did so in keeping with the consensus of Christian authority in his day. Pastorally, the consequence of this answer is simple: infant baptism. If we are sinners from the womb, then from the womb we need redemption. In a world where the infant's grasp on life was tenuous, the urgency was strongly felt. Thus baptism offered immediate forgiveness of original sin and hence the removal of all the eternal penalties for that ancient fault; in addition, the sacrament washed the soul clean of the whole burden of actual sin that might have accumulated, however slight. To die at the moment after baptism was to speed straight to heaven.

Outwardly, the sacrament marked a person's entry into full membership in the church. Thus the child entered the church by an unearned favor, by which the eternal penalties of original sin were removed. Only the actual sins of the individual after baptism could do harm now.

Did Augustine consider baptism necessary for salvation? Yes, with a qualification. From the earliest times, the church had recognized that in certain cases, such as that of the martyrs, the intention was as good as the act. For Augustine, there was little need to speak of the accession of grace to those who had not been baptised, for in the Christian Roman empire the sacrament itself was readily available. Negligence in its reception was the only thing that could ordinarily forestall it.[4]

Practically speaking, baptism was the sacrament that formed the church itself. Catechumens, outsiders contemplating entrance, continued to be only fringe members of the community; it was still the custom to exclude them from the communion service of the liturgy. Baptism, on the other hand, rendered the individual eligible for full sacramental participation in the eucharist and was a necessary prerequisite for any ecclesiastical office.

What was left untouched by baptism was concupiscence, the inclination toward sin that original sin had introduced. The sacrament cleared the slate for the past and offered support for the future, but it was not the end of the story. Sin remained a present possibility for the Christian, and ultimate success was uncertain.

Human life in the church was full of hope, but still devoid of
assurance. Only later in Augustine's life would the precise theological definition of this dilemma (centered on the doctrine of perseverance) come out. For the moment, in the last books of this little
pamphlet of 411, the concern was with life in a world burdened by
sin. Having outlined the theology of original sin and its pastoral
consequences in the first book, Augustine returns to the main topic.
Is original sin universal? Yes. A further question poses itself neatly
enough. Is there now or has there ever been a human being born
alive who was completely without sin, original or actual? One and
one only, according to Augustine: Christ, the exception who literally
proves the rule.[5]

The consequences of this pessimism are spelled out in detail.
First, the ubiquity of sin, even its "inevitability," do not remove
any of the blame for sin. Human beings are not mere puppets on
whom sin is inflicted, rather they are free individuals who, however
mysterious it seems, bear full responsibility for the free act of one
of their ancestors. For this reason, sinlessness is both possible and
impossible. Possible, "through the grace of God and men's own
free will, not doubting that the free will itself is ascribable to God's
grace" (2.6.7), and hence the blame that inheres as a result of sin,
even original sin; but impossible, in the sense that it does not in
fact ever occur.

> There are on earth righteous people, there are great men, brave, prudent,
> chaste, patient, pious, merciful people, who endure all kinds of temporal
> evil with an even mind for righteousness' sake. If, however, there is truth—
> nay, because there is truth—in these words, "If we say we have no sin,
> we deceive ourselves" (1 John 1.8), and in these, "In thy sight shall no
> man living be justified" (Ps. 142.2), they are not without sin. Nor is
> there one among them so proud and foolish as not to think that the Lord's
> Prayer [with its clause, "Forgive us our trespasses"] is needful to him, by
> reason of his manifold sins. (2.3.18)

With this one stroke Augustine makes all Christian statements about
perfection and righteousness partial and tentative. The perfection
of the blessed in this life is not the perfection of heaven. Anything
less than the perfection of heaven contains an element of the sinful.

Why does man not in fact avoid sin, if the possibility is guaranteed
to him? The answer will remind the reader of Augustine's theory
of the origin of sin in *City of God:* "To this question I might very

easily and truthfully answer: Because men are unwilling. But if I am asked why they are unwilling, we are drawn into a lengthy statement. And yet, without prejudice to a more careful examination, I may say briefly this much: Men are unwilling to do what is right, either because what is right is unknown to them, or because it is unpleasant to them" (2.17.26). Argument can go no farther. Men sin because they sin. In this refusal to provide explanations, we can see the freedom of the will that Augustine is eager to protect. Any cause or explanation he might assign for sin would lessen the freedom of the will along with the blame. People are responsible for their sins because they sin freely. The miracle of creation means that beings exist who have this autonomy. The miracle of redemption means that a God exists who brings them back from perdition when they have exercised their autonomy unwisely.

Men are thus separated from God by an awesome sentence that means they are divided from all that gives life and joy. Worse, the separation is entirely of their own doing. Worse still, for a charitable soul, everyone is afflicted with the same separation. Pathetically, even tiny infants are not free from the contagion. The blight is intensely personal. Men are separated from God, and hence are separated from themselves. Not only do nations mistrust and threaten each other, but even small communities are full of suspicion and crime. Not even the family household draws the line against hostility and separation. Division and misery reach right into the heart of every individual. No one can trust even himself fully, for no one is in control of his own acts at all times. We are at war with ourselves.

Into this gloom, the Christian church—to all appearances merely an earthly association of sinners—carries a message of divine salvation and offers a divine act of redemption—not one hidden away in the holy of holies where only the perfect may enter, but one set literally on the doorstep, accessible to all who will humble themselves to accept it. Baptism releases the individual from the worst of chains and initiates the believer into the life of grace. Much that is difficult remains ahead. Only with that beginning is the fact of grace itself intelligible; but beginnings are not to be scorned.

Grace

The ancient religions were relatively consistent in their picture of the world. Divine power, easily angered, surrounded human beings and threatened unspeakable wrath. Prudent people discovered what it took to placate that divinity and sedulously undertook the form of service most pleasing to the divine tyrant. In return, threats vanished and earthly and heavenly delights began to be showered on the faithful votary. Divine favor, moreover, was shown in different degrees for different levels of performance on the part of the human partners to the contract.[6]

Behind this ancient religious system lay a fundamentally incoherent anthropology. For the gap between god and man was radical and scarcely to be crossed save by the heroes of myth. Ordinary mortals were destined to a lifetime (perhaps an eternity) of settling for second best. Even in the afterlife, the gods would remain distant and authoritarian. The best one could hope for was a lessening of threats and dangers, a truce. On the other hand, there was an altogether baseless optimism about the range of human powers. With accurate knowledge about the will of the gods, any intelligent man could immediately (perhaps after a physical rite of purification) set about the task of satisfying the god's desires. Permanently humble, but unremittingly powerful, such was the nature of man.

But Christianity had too high a regard for the power of sin to accept such a view of man's capacities, and too high a regard for the goodness of God to believe in an arbitrary celestial tyrant. Instead of preaching final insignificance but present power, Christianity reversed the polarities and discovered an anthropology pessimistic regarding the capacities of sinful man but optimistic about his fate.

The coming transformation is the result of no innate merit on the part of the species. Sin has pulled mankind so low that no right to divine favor remains. The favor that comes is free and unearned, a gift from above. Men were created to give God praise and honor of their own free will with undarkened intelligence, but they rebelled. They chose ignorance over intelligence and impotence over self-control, but God reached out and pulled them up again.

This is the center of the Augustinian theology of grace. More can be said about the philosophical basis of Augustine's theology of grace and free will, but for the moment it should be kept in mind that for Augustine himself the firm central point was his conviction of the reality of God's power and favor shown to sinful man. If human reason could not understand the workings of this grace, that was deplorable (and Augustine would labor mightily, as none before and few since, to bring about greater understanding), but no failure to understand ever caused Augustine the slightest doubt as to the truth of the doctrine he embraced.

Here, as always, Augustine's theology was fundamentally biblical and his method of argument exegetical. After he had written *The Guilt and Remission of Sin,* the further questions of his friend, the imperial legate Marcellinus, led him to expatiate further on grace itself. He did so in *Spirit and Letter,* whose title reveals the intimate relation between his thought on this subject and his theory of exegesis. This treatise is Augustine's most compact and readable exposition of his theology of grace, and it has the advantage of having been written before the passions of the Pelagian controversy began to direct argument down lines that would ultimately obscure as much as they illuminated.[7]

The question that elicited this treatise is the one that occupied much of the second book of the earlier pamphlet for Marcellinus: can any man be perfectly just in this life? Marcellinus now emphasized the apparent injustice of condemning men for sin if sinlessness is not in their power. Augustine begins by reviewing his explanation that sin is virtually inevitable, but inevitable as a result of earlier sinfulness rather than as a result of an exterior constraint on human actions. This all leads to considering the mechanism by which God deals with man in the Christian dispensation: hence the relevance of the spirit and the letter.

When the intellect encounters revelation, its natural response is to scrutinize the literal sense of the text: the instinct for scholarship runs deep in the species. The text is held at arm's length and analyzed, not clasped to the breast and accepted wholeheartedly. But Augustine believed that to take only the literal sense of the text is the choice of sinful people determined to maintain themselves in sin-begotten autonomy and separation from God. He urges the reader to let the spiritual meaning of the text do its work, evoking the whole of salvation history and the place therein of the individual believer. The relation between spirit and letter, moreover, is characteristically the relation between the New and Old Testaments. The Jewish people of old had the words of God in their Law, but they read those words literally and obeyed them punctiliously. Christianity proposed an alternative spiritual reading of that Old Testament history.

Thus, the function of the law of the Old Testament was not to enact a law whose precise observance could win an eternal reward.

Rather the law was to reveal to mankind its iniquities—nothing more: "Through the Law came an awareness of sin" (Rom. 3.20). The proper response to the law is remorse and repentance and a longing for divine aid. To take the law as a complete and exclusive set of commandments leading to perfection is the sin of the pharisees. But Augustine, expounding Paul, is so clear on these points that he should be allowed to speak for himself:

> The apostle wanted to commend the grace that has come to all nations through Jesus Christ, lest the Jews should boast of themselves at the expense of other peoples on account of their having the Law. First he says that sin and death came on the human race through one man [Adam], and that righteousness and eternal life came also through one [Christ]. Then he adds that "the law entered, that sin might abound. But where sin abounded, grace did much more abound, so that as sin hath reigned unto death, even so might grace reign through righteousness unto eternal life by Jesus Christ our Lord" (Rom. 5.20–21). . . . For there was need to prove to man how corruptly weak he was. Against his iniquity, the holy law brought him no help towards good, but increased rather than diminished his iniquity, for the law entered that sin might abound. Thus convicted and confounded, man might see that he needed not only a physician, but even God as his helper to direct his steps so sin would not rule over him, and so he might be healed by fleeing to the aid of divine mercy. In this way, where sin abounded grace might much more abound, not through the merit of the sinner, but by the intervention of his helper. (6.9)

An end is called, therefore, to all bargaining for salvation. Man is not a free, strong, and independent (but subordinate) being dealing with a powerful adversary. He is a helpless, self-shackled creature, first acknowledging error in the face of the law, then accepting the free gift of redemption through the grace of the New Testament. This is the deepest meaning of the duality of the testaments.

> What difference there is between the old covenant and the new is therefore obvious. In the former the law is written on tablets, while in the latter it is written on hearts. . . . In the one man becomes a transgressor through the letter that kills, in the other a lover through the life-giving spirit. We must therefore avoid saying that God assists us to work righteousness and "works in us both to will and to do of his good pleasure" (Phil. 2.13), by addressing to us external commands of holiness. For he

gives his increase internally, by shedding love abroad in our hearts by the holy spirit that is given to us. (25.42)

The apparent pattern of salvation history breaks down. Christ did not come simply to revise and update (with perhaps some generous simplifications) the commands of the Old Testament. Christianity does not simply humanize the monotheism of Judaism. Where in the pre-Christian view, God is typically somewhere outside and above, now for the Christian, God is also within the individual, exercising a transforming power regardless of human merits.

This power is one that the subjects of the transformation, ordinary men and women, find difficult to understand. Our deepest assumption is that we are here somehow all by ourselves, part of a society to be sure, but still intrinsically ourselves alone. But Augustine and Paul show us that we are opaque to ourselves. The conflict of wills and instincts in man seem somehow alien, but it is not. The will to goodness and, where it exists, the power to achieve that will are not man's but are the effect of the lord and creator of the universe personally working within man, so far within that the mechanics of the process elude perception. For Augustine, for his church, and for much of late antique thought, the inner man is more and more the focus of mystery and the locus of conflict.

Grace is not a gift present to all men in the same way, which some choose to accept and some reject. If this were the case, the gift would lose its power, and salvation would be distributed in accordance with the merit of having accepted the gift. Where grace prevails, it does so regardless of the choice of the individual subjected to it. The paradox is that moral responsibility for rejecting God remains, while the moral merit for accepting God is abolished by grace. This creates a two-fold system of judgment in appearance, whereby it is just for God to punish the damned and merciful for him to reward the blessed, and not at all inconsistent to treat the two groups differently. Those unable to live with paradox are driven either to a harsh system of double predestination or to a generous doctrine of final blessedness for all. Augustine, always sensitive to paradox, had, as we shall see, a more complex response.

Pelagius held, apparently, that grace as spoken of in scripture consisted of the good nature given to all men (which even sin only taints but does not destroy) and of revelation given through Christ. Men are given a basic goodness and the knowledge to employ that goodness. Their reaction then is their own free and responsible choice, by which they earn or fail to earn eternal salvation. But for Augustine, nature and grace are always two different things. The Pelagian analysis works if applied to Adam and Eve, perhaps, but they chose badly and fell from the state of preternatural grace that was theirs by nature. In a world vitiated by their sin, a second order of divine generosity was needed if men were to be saved. The supernatural grace of Christ's redemption is special medicine to heal a fallen world, and it works in special ways. Grace cannot simply be reduced to God's sense of fair play.

This grace, then, is absolute. It forestalls all merit, instructs the sinner concerning what is right, gives the power to do what is right, and is itself mysteriously the act of doing what is right. What men do that is wrong, they do themselves; what they do that is right, God does in them.

This system would seem to leave little room for free will. Human beings are either sinners or puppets. The controversy Augustine fought on this point developed over a decade, but it is important to see what Augustine had to say at the outset, in *Spirit and Letter*. "Do we then by grace make void free will? God forbid! No! Rather we establish free will. For even as the law by faith, so free will by grace, is not made void, but strengthened. The law is fulfilled only by free will, but from the law comes knowledge of sin, from faith the acquisition of grace against sin, from grace the healing of the soul from the disease of sin, from the health of the soul freedom of will, from free will the love of righteousness, from love of righteousness the accomplishment of the law" (30.52).

True freedom of the will is the highest and noblest of human faculties, but it can be seriously damaged and even destroyed by its own self-inflicted wounds. When Adam and Eve encountered the divine command about the tree in the garden, then and then only was the freedom of choice absolute. But all choices have moral effects, and only the good choices are compatible with freedom of the will. God is absolutely good, and all that is less than God is inherently less good. Turning the will from what is best to what is less good places constraints on that will itself, constraints from which it cannot then loose itself. Left to itself, the will that has chosen wrongly continues to choose wrongly, and its freedom is damaged by its own act. Divine grace, on the other hand, provides redemption from the self-inflicted loss of freedom and restores the will to the original state of freedom. Obviously, none of this is as simple as Augustine made it seem in *Spirit and Letter,* but he saw it just that clearly. The clarity of that vision inspired all his later writing.

One consequence of this doctrine is that the final redemption of the soul is a matter for heavenly judgment to determine. Christ brings redemption and establishes a church by which redemption is mediated, but this church has no magic power. This is no pagan mystery religion, initiation in which brings automatic redemption once for all. Augustine was intensely aware of the power of ecclesiastically mediated grace to bring about miracles of moral reformation and of the lingering power of sin to reclaim even those who had seemed on the road to salvation. He spoke once of the example of the elderly man who had lived for decades chastely and continently in the peace of the church, but then suddenly and inexplicably in old age took up with a young woman and abandoned his earlier life of righteousness.[8]

Augustine holds therefore that divine grace works both absolutely and by degrees. Faith and baptism mark the first stage on a long road. With divine assistance that road will be followed to its end, but if the assistance fails, failure remains possible. The liberation of the will from the shackles of sin is only partial, and constant relapse in small matters is inevitable, just as total relapse in large matters is possible. The Christian life is a constant struggle—but not of the kind Pelagius imagined. It is not that men struggle with vice—it is that divine grace struggles to overcome the inner tendency to turn away. Pride on the other side struggles constantly to defeat virtue.

This principle finally answers the question that began *Spirit and Letter.* Even for the baptised Christian living in evident harmony with the precepts of Christ and the church, perfection of righteousness is nowhere to be found on earth. Perfection may be spoken of, but only as a prefiguration, bearing as much (and as little) resemblance to the perfection of the blessed as the outward appearance of Jesus, the carpenter's son, bears to Christ, the risen Lord, seated in glory at the right hand of the Father.

This great paradox cleaves the world in half, leaving an endless array of lesser paradoxes in its wake. Throughout his writings of this period, Augustine constantly iterates his belief both in the paradoxical quality of the doctrine he has to preach and in the ultimate resolution of those paradoxes in divine knowledge. *Spirit and Letter* ends with a scriptural quotation that runs like a *leit-motif* through the anti-Pelagian writings of Augustine.[9] As we prepare to turn to his elucidation of the deepest paradoxes of freedom and predestination, it will be useful to see this quotation ending this section, just as Augustine used it to conclude *Spirit and Letter*. Grave pitfalls await any controversialist who enters the lists against Augustine without appreciating the significance of these ideas. He introduces the crucial passage by another quotation from Paul:

"My grace is sufficient for thee; for my strength is made perfect in weakness" (2 Cor. 12.7–9). A fixed and certain reason remains, therefore, in the hidden depths of God's judgments, why every mouth, even of the righteous, should be shut in its own praise, and opened only for the praise of God. But what this reason is, who can unearth, who can investigate, who can know? So "unsearchable are his judgments, and his ways past finding out! For who hath known the mind of the Lord? Or who hath been his counselor? Or who hath first given to him, that it shall be repaid to him again? For of him, and through him, and to him, are all things: to whom be glory forever, Amen." (Rom. 11.33–36)

Free Will

Readers with little taste for paradox find many frustrations in Augustine. Those frustrations are about to come to a peak. For the fallen human intellect to understand the workings of divine salvation is, for Augustine, a task destined to glorious failure. Failure, because such understanding will be incomplete, but glorious, because the more intensely that failure is realized, the closer the knowing person comes to God.[10]

To begin with, as always for Augustine, there is God. To God, all that transpires is intelligible and reasonable. God is omniscient, but also omnipotent. All that is, is of God; creation is encompassed by God and dwarfed by him. Appearances are only complicated shadows cast by simple realities we will never fully comprehend. Human beings, created in the image and likeness of God, possess the faculty of reason, and in theory nothing should prevent them from sharing divine knowledge. But in practice something does interfere. Sin leads to ignorance and misunderstanding, and in this life grace itself leads only to partial and incomplete restoration of the intellect.

But human beings pretend otherwise. They perceive small fragments of the reasonableness of divine creation and think they know
the whole story. They grasp a piece of the truth and identify it with
the whole. Then attention is drawn to a crucial theological puzzle,
a system of logic fails to resolve all the issues that are raised, and
scapegoats are sought. Men blame the system, blame the puzzle,
blame God himself, but never blame themselves.

The problems raised by Augustine's theology of sin and grace
and its limitations were thrust upon him with most painful force
in the last decade of his life, when some monks in Africa and Gaul,
concerned that the value of their own self-denying way of life was
undermined by what they saw as defeatist quietism, began propa-
gating ideas that have received in modern times the inaccurate name
of "semi-Pelagianism." (The discussion with the ascetics of Gaul
and Africa provides a more fruitful discussion for our purposes than
does the rancorous contemporaneous quarrel between Augustine and
Julian of Eclanum, though the issues are similar.) The conclusion
they reached was that God's grace is a reward for well-intentioned
initial efforts by human beings.[11] In other words, some limited role
for human merit remains at the root of the theology of salvation.
What matters about this opposition is not so much its conclusions
as the line of reasoning that led to the dispute.

The monks observed that a thoroughgoing system of divine grace
leads to logical difficulties. If grace is absolutely sovereign and
human merit entirely nonexistent, does not freedom of the will
disappear? Worse, does it not mean that it is God who chooses,
not only who will go to heaven, but also who will go to hell? Cannot
those who go to hell rightly blame the negligence and cruelty of a
God who denied them the free gift given to others just as unde-
serving? Can God be just if such whimsy reigns? Is God really
merciful?

A related question attacks the problem neatly: Is grace resistible?
This would seem to suggest an attractive escape route, for if grace
is resistible, then those who are damned are responsible for their
own damnation. But if the answer to this question is affirmative,
we must ask whether that means that grace is also acceptable; that
is, if it is in the power of human beings to reject it, is it not also
in their power to accept it? And has not merit returned to the
system? If it is not in our power to accept grace, but only to reject
it, the justice and mercy of God remain in question, for God must

foreordain which people will be allowed to resist and which will be compelled to accept—and divine whimsy, a terrifying notion, re-enters.

Augustine does not have a simple, comprehensive solution acceptable to all for these dilemmas. His principle, as in the question of original sin, is to cling to what he knows for certain, to attempt to provide explanations for difficulties, but then to stand with what he knows by faith even when logical difficulties remain. Here, as always, revelation and experience are everything for Augustine; the arguments of the dialecticians have no authority.

With those warnings, we can turn with trepidation to the Augustinian solution. Augustine believes in predestination, but only in single predestination. God actively chooses certain individuals to be the recipients of his grace, confers it on them in a way that altogether overpowers their own will to sin, and leaves them utterly transformed, to live a life of blessedness. But God does not choose beforehand to send others to hell. God wills that all men be saved (cf. 1 Tim. 2.4) even as he takes actions that save only certain individuals. Those who are damned are damned by their own actions.

On these points Augustine will not be shaken. His opponents (and a fair number of would-be friends) through the centuries will insist that this solution is indistinguishable from double predestination. It will be claimed that this view is pessimistic and proclaims a tyrannical and arbitrary God. Psychology will be invoked to explain the growing gloom of the aging Augustine.

Before we judge Augustine, however, we should attempt to understand him. He knew his answer could only be half a solution. Evil and its sources were still wrapped in mystery for him as the manifestation of nonbeing in the world of being. Augustine can only attempt to explain the workings of God and his goodness, which are clear and intelligible. To understand the condition of the evil creatures who will not win eternal blessedness is painfully difficult. All this makes hard doctrine.

If the divine deliberation by which some are saved and some are damned is a mystery, however, something less obscure can be said about the condition of the will of the redeemed creature. We must consider for a moment the nature of the faculty of will itself.[12]

In practical terms, it is scarcely too strong to say that the will is the personality. The will is the part of the soul that chooses and acts. All choices are choices of will, and all acts are acts of appetite, hence acts of love, either the divinely inspired love Augustine calls *caritas*, or the sinful selfish love he calls *cupiditas*. Personal, conscious existence is not somewhere outside the instrumental faculty we call will, rationally deliberating how to employ that faculty to achieve its ends. Instead, existence, knowledge, and will are an indissociable whole, and all deliberation and choice is of the will—of love. Given this psychology, it is then logical to argue that the power of sin over the individual must be considered when freedom is assessed. The will is always free of external control. There is no such thing as a compelled act for Augustine, one that goes "against the will." Even when we are "compelled" to do something, it is only that the conditions in which the will freely operates are altered.

So freedom of the will from external constraint is always absolute. Its freedom becomes impaired when it begins to choose the wrong kind of love and so to bind itself to inferior choices in a self-perpetuating, self-damning process. When divine grace intervenes, it liberates the individual from the bondage of wrong past choices. Precisely how this happens is a little unclear to Augustine, but it is clear that God, without ever tampering with the interior working of the will itself, can still direct its choices by altering, in perfect omniscience, the circumstances that affect the will.

The whole process of grace is seen by God, eternally knowing all things, as a single unity, but it appears to men as a series, sometimes a lifelong series, of events no one of which necessarily entails any further event. Thus when human beings speak of grace, they speak imperfectly. God's grace cannot be said to be working in the life of an individual even when that individual is destined, at a later date, to rebel, fall into sin, and choose damnation. Augustine describes this process best in another late treatise, *The Gift of Perseverance*. From a human point of view, the divine grace that effects salvation is best described as Initial Grace plus the Grace of Perseverance. From the divine point of view, it is better to say that unless the Grace of Perseverance is present, the Initial Grace is not finally grace at all but only some lesser gift.

The best way to see this process would be from the point of view of heaven. The blessed soul, from the moment of first turning to God, lives in a state of constant indeterminacy. Grace brings many gifts of consolation and strength, but each day brings new trials and the need for new gifts. Whether the gifts will in the end match the trials will not be known until the sorting out of the sheep from the goats at the last judgment. This predestination appears in the world under most uncertain guise.

Practically, therefore, the life of the Christian is lived on the horns of a dilemma. Grace must be firmly believed to be omnipotent; without grace nothing good can be done. All that is good in the soul must come from God, while all that is bad is of one's own doing. And yet all this appears to the individual as a matter of individual choices of that frustratingly free will. The faithful Christian, therefore, is one who believes utterly in God but who responds to the exigencies of daily life by living as though everything, salvation included, depends on his own actions. God is all-powerful and predestining, but the will is free, and the one who believes and hopes in God must act as though for himself, but act out of a completely disinterested, selfless love—*caritas, not cupiditas.*

Nowhere does Augustine suggest that any of this is easy. The Christian is keenly aware of the ambivalences of earthly existence and feels strongly the dilemmas of living as an isolated individual subject to a commandment that requires him to think himself part of a completely selfless and loving community. The damned can live in the world as they see it, but the blessed are doomed to live, for the time being, in two worlds, one of appearances, one of realities. In the world of appearances, they cannot avoid sin; but in the world of reality, they must avoid it. In the world of appearances, they have freedom of choice clear and simple, which they use for sin; in the world of reality, freedom of choice is transformed utterly into a genuine freedom, which in fact chooses only the good and hence looks (in the world of appearances) like something less than total freedom. All the while, the evil flourish. Selfishness does turn out to be a remarkably efficient way to go about living in the here and now—for the strong and the lucky.

This doctrine of the will deals with the central mystery of human existence, the question of who we are and what we are here for. Augustine's answer had to be confusing and obscure to many, perhaps finally and irrationally paradoxical even to the best-intentioned of readers. But Augustine never wavered in maintaining this difficult position. Instead he kept quoting Paul on the unsearchable judgments of God. He never let it escape his attention that when the choice must be made between divine goodness and human reason, the choice must be for God, not for man. That the problem remained ultimately insoluble was for him in a sense merely evidence that

God was still God and man, fallen but on the way to redemption, was still man.

One further irony must be faced. The dilemmas of predestination create an urgent sense of frustration by the absence of clear, logically compelling answers. Believers wonder at the ineptitude of the theologians, while skeptics take the failure of the Christians to settle the problem as evidence of the incoherence of the creed. The irony is that both positions are correct, but neither is complete. For what is most significant is precisely that insistence of the human mind on being given a straight answer. The human mind, here and now, naturally expects all problems to have solutions. Men expect, even demand, to make sense of the world. But that quality of the human mind is, to Augustine, a proud and Pelagian trait. The intellect does not willingly yield its control over action. Rebellion and skepticism are more characteristic, as is evident from (and explained by, Augustine would say) the story of Adam and Eve.

The Pelagian position on Christianity is finally a pagan one. God creates the world and issues his commands. Men are to learn the commands, obey them, and so win salvation. The situation is simple, requiring merely that the rules be clear and intelligible and devoid of paradox and confusion. The entire Augustinian system is radically opposed to this. That God appears to us as a master of paradox tells him something about mankind, but nothing about God. Faith, which is what grace instills in the heart, is the assertion that God is God, despite the paradoxes that make him seem arbitrary, unjust, or mysterious. For Augustine, God was always God, he was himself always a sinner, and paradox and mystery were the price he had to pay.

Chapter Five
Augustine

Noverim me, noverim te: "I would know myself, I would know you [God]."[1] Augustine wrote these words in one of his earliest works, but they retained their force throughout his lifetime.[2] The irrefutable solipsism of self confronted with the absolute reality of God, the wholly other: all of Augustine's thought moves between those two poles.

But those poles were not far distant from one another, with vast uncharted territory between. Rather, they were elements of an intimate personal relationship destined for permanent and indissoluble union. To treat God and self as two different things is to introduce the fatal distinction that the serpent taught to Eve. The relation between creator and creature is totally different from that which obtains between any two created things in the material world. Each created object participates in a complex world of material objects from which God seems far away. But the creator is equidistant from all creatures—equally close to all.

Theologians write about God dispassionately and objectively, in serene detachment, but in doing so avail themselves of a compendious device that runs the risk of negating the truth of all they say. Christian theology only succeeds when the believer sees that the story of all creation ("macrotheology") and the private history of the soul ("microtheology") are identical. Differences between the two are flaws of perception, not defects inherent in things.

Saints do not have to be taught this identity, for theology realized is holiness. But even saints, when they are theologians, often find it hard to embody their intuition in their works. For Augustine the crisis came early in life. Despite his reputation as a self-revelatory writer, he left behind little direct testimony about the condition of his soul at different times, but we can see that the first years of his episcopacy were a time of trial. He had managed the transformation from virtual pagan to devout Christian with reasonable equanimity. The map for that conversion was clear enough and commonly followed. Even his elevation to the priesthood in the church of Hippo had brought with it few fresh anxieties.

But the final elevation to the bishopric seems to have unsteadied Augustine a bit. The transition was accompanied by some jibing from outside—suspicions of his Manichean past, rumor of an illicit connection with a married woman, jealousy from some less-educated African churchmen toward this well-educated outsider rising too rapidly to the top. Those things, however, must have been only the surface disturbances. Augustine was more deeply troubled by the implications of his new office.

Who was he to stand in such a place of eminence, with so many people depending on him? He was still a sinner, but somehow he was also the conduit of divine grace bringing redemption to other sinners. Now a preacher, he needed to be preached to himself, but there was no one to do that. He had to stand alone before the people of Hippo each week and proclaim God's word. How could the expectations of these people not drive him to despair?

Two literary answers came out of this personal crisis. The first was perfectly theological, detached, and serious: *Christian Doctrine* was begun, and carried out through most of the third book, in the year or so after his elevation to the bishopric. In it, as we have seen, Augustine sketched dispassionately the nature of the Christian message and the mechanism of its proclamation to the world. It was a handbook for others who would preach, but it was a personal statement of intent as well. How do I preach, he asked himself. *Christian Doctrine* was the answer. But it was an incomplete answer, in more ways than one. At about this time he turned instead to writing the *Confessions*.

Detachment and objectivity are not to be found in the *Confessions*. Analysis of divine affairs is not only not kept apart from self-analysis, but the two streams are run together in what often appears to first readers to be an uncontrolled and illogical mélange. This book's fascination for modern readers stems in large part from its vivid portrayal of a man in the presence of his God, of God and the self intimately related but still separated by sin, and of a struggle for mastery within the self longing for final peace. It is an extraordinary book, no matter how studied.

The rest of Augustine's life was spent writing books of a more conventional sort. He would analyze in painstaking detail the inner workings of the trinity, the whole course of salvation history, and

the delicate commerce between God and man in the workings of
grace and the will, all in an objective, detached, and impersonal
style.[3] What is different about them is that they were written by
a man who had already written the *Confessions*, made his peace with
God insofar as that was possible, and drawn from that peace (the
forerunner of heavenly rest) the confidence he needed to stand at
the altar and preach or to sit in his study dictating works of polemic
and instruction for the world to read.

The reading of the *Confessions* given in this chapter, then, may
seem somewhat strange. The *Confessions* are not to be read merely
as a look back at Augustine's spiritual development; rather the text
itself is an essential stage in that development, and a work aware
both of what had already passed into history and of what lay ahead.
No other work of Christian literature does what Augustine accom-
plishes in this volume; only Dante's *Commedia* even rivals it.

Prayer—so all the authoritative writers state—is no simple matter. It is not easy to pray. In view of that, we should direct our
first attention to the form of Augustine's masterwork and portion
out at least some of our admiration for his accomplishment of a very
difficult task: praying on paper. The literary form of the work is a
continuous address to God. No human audience is directly addressed, although in Book 10 Augustine will wonder what such an
audience might make of the work. But at all times the direction of
the work is toward God.

Such a work would seem doomed to failure. Prayer is private,
but literature is unfailingly public; prayer is humble, but literature
is always a form of self-assertion; prayer is intimate, but literature
is voyeuristic. One might be able to depict another's prayer suc-
cessfully (for then the voyeurism and the self-assertion are the responsibility of the author, not of the individual at prayer), except
that no third party can ever enter into the privacy of another's relation
with God.

But somehow or other Augustine succeeds. The *Confessions* are
marked by an unfailing consistency of tone and authenticity of style.
The believer and the writer function as one, with no awkwardness
or embarrassment. There is never a false note, no false modesty, no
posing for an audience. We come away convinced that, whatever
else we have learned, in it we have seen Augustine at prayer, as he
was.

We need not insist that Augustine prayed in the privacy of his cell with just such words, just such cadences, just such nuanced and orderly allusions to scripture, just such unfailing intensity. The text is not the private prayer of a man on his knees in a chapel. In fact, in the *Confessions* Augustine succeeded at something even more difficult than transcribing his private devotions accurately. He has instead devised an idiom by which it is possible to pray in a literary medium, that is, to pray as one would have to pray with pen in hand. This text does not represent Augustine's prayer life as signifier represents signified; the text is itself the thing signified, the very prayer itself, the act of communication between Augustine and God. Its relation to the rest of Augustine's prayer life is not as snapshot to subject but as one subject to another.

The implications of this literary form come to be the subject of the *Confessions* themselves in the tenth book. We must bear in mind that we are not reading a book of any ordinary kind. This is emphatically not the "first modern autobiography," for the autobiographical narrative that takes up part of the work is incidental content while prayer is the significant form. The work is sui generis.

Sin

The *Confessions* begin as prayer. The first few pages are dense and abstract, but they are of deep significance to the whole work and to Augustine's life, and they repay study. The beginning is abrupt— and not Augustine's. *"Great art Thou, O Lord, and greatly to be praised; great is Thy power, and Thy wisdom infinite."* These lines juxtapose and combine two Psalm texts (144[145].3 and 146[147].5). With them, Augustine embodies his own principle from *Christian Doctrine*, that he who speaks of religion should rely on the language of scripture itself. Though necessity often compels the believer to use his own words, constant recourse to the very words of scripture provides a safety net over which the speculative theologian and confused penitent may work.

The content of these lines is praise: a humble mortal enunciates the greatness of God, greatness of action and contemplation, of power and wisdom, embracing all that is. That greatness is in fact "greatly to be praised." Much of the *Confessions* will sound the same laudatory note, and not by accident. We ordinarily interpret "confession" as a single-valued term, acknowledgment of wrongdoing by a miscreant. But the etymology has simply to do with emphatic agreement or acknowledgment. Confession of sin is the negative form of confession. Confession of praise, on the other hand, is the acknowledgment by the creature of the greatness and goodness of God. Confession of faith is then emphatic assent to a set of facts about God and God's relation to mankind.

All three confessions occur in the *Confessions*.[4] If God and the soul are all Augustine wants to know, and if they are to be known best in relation to each other, then acknowledgment of the weakness of the individual and of the power and greatness of God are two sides of the same coin. Sinful man sets himself in God's place; confession of sin demolishes that preposterousness. Sinful man belittles God's power at the expense of his own; confession of praise restores God's place in the sinner's eyes. Confession of faith declares what has transpired to the community of believers. Seen this way, confession is the working out of redemption itself in the life of the sinner. It is prayer itself. The literary text, prayer on paper, becomes in this way again not a picture of the working out of Augustine's salvation, but the instrument of salvation itself.

> And Thee would a man praise;
> a man, but a particle of Thy creation;
> a man, that bears about him his mortality,
> the witness of sin,
> the witness, that *Thou resistest the proud:*
> yet would a man praise Thee;
> he, but a particle of Thy creation.

God is great, but man is tiny, yet man, full of sin and death and rejection, somehow or another reaches up, as improbable as it may seem, to praise God. This is preposterous, but unavoidable.

> Thou awakest us to delight in Thy praise;
> for Thou madest us for Thyself,
> and our heart is restless, until it rests in Thee.

This most famous line in the *Confessions* is also an accurate summary of its contents. The natural motion of the spirit is from the restlessness of alienation from God to the repose of peace and union with God. The *Confessions,* among many other things, follow this path from restlessness to peace itself. (A glance ahead at the last

words on the last page of the *Confessions* [13.35–38] will confirm
this.) In the beginning, confusion and division; in the end, peace.

> Grant me, Lord, to know and understand which is first,
> to call on Thee or to praise Thee?
> and, again, to know Thee or to call on Thee?
> For who can call on Thee, not knowing Thee?
> For he that knoweth Thee not,
> may call on Thee as other than Thou art.
> Or is it rather,
> that we call on Thee that we may know Thee?

How does praise come about? Is it man's doing? But if it is his
doing, how is it not inevitable—for if all can know God, all would
praise him, would they not? The precise sequence of Augustine's
question is this: In what order do the apparently separate acts occur
of knowing God, appealing to God, and praising God? Does not
knowledge have to come first? (For without knowledge, we would
not know on whom we were to call or whom to praise.) Or is perhaps
that we pray first, in order to gain knowledge? Augustine himself
began by calling on the name of God, but now he seeks knowledge
(the word he uses is one he uses elsewhere in similar contexts as a
name for faith) and understanding. The answer to the question comes
from the source of all answers.

> But *how shall they call on Him*
> *in whom they have not believed?*
> *or how shall they believe without a preacher?*
> And *they that seek the Lord shall praise Him.*
> For *they that seek shall find Him,*
> and they that find shall praise Him.

Scripture provides in this conflation of several passages answers to
all the questions.[5] Invocation requires belief (faith) first; belief requires a preacher; praise comes after seeking and is indeed part of
a sequence that runs seeking-finding-praising. Given these data,
Augustine can answer his questions in rational order.

> I will seek Thee, Lord, by calling on Thee;
> and will call on Thee, believing in Thee;
> for to us hast Thou been preached.

> My faith, Lord, shall call on Thee,
> which Thou hast given me,
> wherewith Thou hast inspired me,
> through the incarnation of Thy Son,
> through the ministry of the preacher.

Here is the essence: faith calls on God (seeking-finding-praising: that sequence follows necessarily on calling on God, as we are left to deduce), but faith comes from outside the individual, through the second person of the trinity.

Thus God is great, and mankind (though outwardly insignificant) is capable of praising God, but this capacity is no accomplishment of man himself. God preaches his Word to man, which results in faith, which results in invocation, which results in seeking, which results in finding, which results in praise. So the economy of the Christian experience is defined: faith is the beginning, unceasing praise (in heaven) is the end, and human life is a journey from faith to praise, from restlessness to repose. God is the guiding force, drawing men to himself despite their unworthiness.

Faith is thus the ground whence invocation rises. The next paragraphs deal with the problem of invocation. What can it possibly mean to "call on God?" This puzzle becomes the means by which Augustine expresses awe and reverence at the majesty of God in a vivid, overtowering depiction of God, full of paradox:

> What art Thou then, my God?
> What, but the Lord God?
> *For who is Lord but the Lord?*
> *or who is God save our God?*
> Most highest, most good, most potent, most omnipotent;
> most merciful, yet most just;
> most hidden, yet most present;
> most beautiful, yet most strong;
> stable, yet incomprehensible;
> unchangeable, yet all-changing;
> never new, never old;
> all-renewing,
> and *bringing age upon the proud and they know it not;*
> ever working, ever at rest;
> still gathering, yet lacking nothing;
> supporting, filling, and overspreading;

creating, nourishing, and maturing;
seeking, yet having all things.
Thou lovest, without passion;
art jealous, without anxiety;
repentest, yet grievest not;
art angry, yet serene;
changest Thy works, Thy purpose unchanged;
receivest again what Thou findest,
yet didst never lose. . . .

(1.4.4)

Intellectually speaking, then, this book is a search for understanding. On this point a little clarification is perhaps useful. Augustine, and the early Latin Middle Ages in general, recognized a
dual epistemology—an ideal theory of knowledge, and a practical
one. In the ideal world, God is known from the glory of creation
itself. Human reason suffices to deduce his existence, and full understanding of the deepest truths is accessible to all. But for fallen
man, sin intervenes. Revelation supplements creation as a source of
knowledge, and the authority of the church supplements faltering
human reason. What revelation and authority give is faith, simple
faith, and the restlessness with which Augustine begins. As the
spirit of grace works, the strength comes to move from the epistemology of the fallen world (and the faith it provides) to the
epistemology of unfallen man (of the Garden of Eden—almost of
heaven) and the direct understanding—mystical contemplation is
perhaps a better term—that comes with it.

The *Confessions* open in faith and restless confusion. This work
will show something of how Augustine proceeded a little way from
faith to understanding and will itself, as literary text, be one of
those steps. Perfect understanding (perfect repose) is impossible this
side of the grave, but every step of the journey is an image of the
whole journey (salvation history is the same story at all times in
every place), and the text that begins with faith in Book 1 and ends
with rest in Book 13 can itself be part of the process described (a
part of the whole whose every part is the whole—paradox on paradox).

A work that begins at the beginning of personal salvation aptly
begins with the beginning of life. Augustine is justly famous for
the insight he brings in these pages of the *Confessions* to the dilemmas
of infancy, even if his sober conclusions seem harsh to us now. The

justice of much of what he says cannot be denied, and when once
we realize where he begins, it is hard to deny him his conclusions.
To Augustine sin is always unprincipled self-assertion. What
seems mere instinct for survival in the beasts of the wild is in human
beings a turning away from love of God and neighbor toward pride
and emptiness. The innocence of small children, Augustine says, is
chiefly inability in their selfishness to wield effective power over
other people's lives. But self-interest, and nothing more, is what
motivates the first attempts to communicate and the first faltering
steps. The infant's love for its parents is not *caritas* at all, for it is
all demanding and no giving.

But the speechless days of infancy are only prologue to Augustine's
recollections. In the first book of the *Confessions* he paints a picture
of himself that highlights the contradictions of his youth. It is a
society no longer faithful to the old traditions but insufficiently sure
of its own mind to devote itself fully to the new religion that we
see reflected in Augustine's religious history. Throughout his early
life, Augustine had a powerful yen to believe. Through wanderings
and confusions, he was constantly on the brink of committing himself to some lofty ideal. Sometimes he even made the gesture. Already as a child, when illness seemed life-threatening, he cried out
for baptism (1.1.17) and almost got his wish, except that his unexpected recovery seemed to render the saving bath unnecessary for
the time.

But at times religious affiliation could mean less to Augustine
than the "natural" inclinations of fallen man. He is not minutely
revelatory of his indiscretions and transgressions, but his self-analysis
suggests at least the shape of his temptations and his lapses. What
information he offers, though, comes almost offhandedly and gives
us little idea of the quality of feeling and emotion that made his
liaisons plausible.

Instead, when he wants to penetrate the depths of his own in-
iquity, he describes the theft of a few pears from a neighbor's tree
(2.4–9). This narrative is placed in his sixteenth year, an idle time
spent at home, his education interrupted by penury, his energies
at the disposal of his fancies. An unflattering portrayal of his father's
reaction to his new maturity shows that it was a time when the
powers of the flesh were beginning to flourish. Then suddenly we
have him and a few friends snatching pears. To ask whether the
theft is meant to represent symbolically the sexual indiscretions of

youth is literal-minded, but some broad analogy at least is probably implied. Although the moral consciousness begins to function in childhood, it is with adolescence and adulthood that the trivial indiscretions of childhood begin to harden into ugly excrescences of moral insensitivity. The adolescent is father to the man. Of that much at least Augustine meant to speak when he chose the pear theft for his meditation on sin.

In speaking of the pears, he strips away irrelevancies and focuses on the sinfulness of the sin. Most immoral acts are undertaken with a purpose—or at least a rationalization—that is at least in part expressly moral. Some innate, positive attraction of the act draws the individual. Even so morally austere an author as Dante could portray the love of Paolo and Francesca with sympathy for a fall that had come through excess of love and enthusiasm; Augustine could well have recounted his own amours at least as deftly. But there was nothing at all redeeming about the theft of the pears. The pears themselves were paltry and unattractive, and the thieves did not even keep them; the comrades with whom he made the theft were not particularly his friends, nor did he want their approval; what attracted him was simply the thrill of the theft itself: forbidden fruit.

Surely Augustine never expected to be cast down to hell for a few pears. But at the same time he felt with awe and horror that the obscure craving that had led him to the pears was the sort of desire by which hell is chosen. To delight in evil for its own sake, to assert one's own primacy in the world by arrogating other's goods to oneself for whatever purpose—there is the embodiment of all evil. The second book of the *Confessions* ends with Augustine facing his own adolescent act in all its trivial magnitude:

Who can disentangle that twisted and intricate knottiness? Foul is it: I hate to think on it, to look on it. . . . I sank away from Thee, and I wandered, my God, too much astray from Thee my stay, in these days of my youth, and I became to myself a barren land. (2.10.18)

The sins of manhood follow upon those of adolescence with dreary inevitability. Despite his preoccupation with himself (perhaps because of it) the world did not reject Augustine, and his career began to offer hint of future glories. As he began to make his way in the world, the tensions that had marked his childhood took on new forms and created new anxieties. He was beginning a life as teacher and student of ancient literature, committed to the propagation of the ancient ideas about man, nature, and the divine that were rooted in the literary tradition. Cicero was his favorite guide in these years, and it was the *Hortensius* of Cicero's that was the spur to all his searches for truth.

But the life of philosophy that this devotee of the classics actually found for himself would not have been highly regarded by Cicero. Augustine took up with the Manichees and pursued the life of perfection it offered. Manicheism was a self-absorbed movement on the periphery of Christianity that crossed the line separating church from cult. It seemed to offer a more rational, scientific picture of the world than did the simple—Augustine may have thought superstitious—orthodox teachings. Augustine had many reasons to find this sect attractive, for in it he found surcease from the plagues of an obviously troubled conscience. Bad conscience can easily turn to neurotic obsession, but Augustine did not remain a convinced Manichee long enough. Rationalism cannot substitute for reason, and the intellectual shoddiness of Manicheism soon turned him away.

Augustine was left leading a curious double life. In public, he was a teacher and a defender of the established order. In private, he was a half-hearted member of an illegal cult whose promises he did not quite credit. For the time being, the headlong rush of his career carried him unthinkingly along. The only qualms he had were instilled (he later thought) by his mother, Monica.

We cannot tell, with the evidence we have, what Monica meant for Augustine before his conversion. He could not have said for certain himself. In the *Confessions* he attributed much to her early influence. His narratives indicate equally that her influence was much ignored and resisted at this period. She wanted to see him a Christian, but he never responded directly to her wish. Christianity itself he scorned, for being too familiar and pedestrian. Only when he had taken a long journey through the exotic underside of late Roman religious life could he return to Christianity and find in it something adequately unfamiliar to carry promise of a happy future. He may well have thought, in early manhood, no more than that Christianity was a good religion for women of little education, like his mother; clever young men could do better for themselves.

The successes of his career mounted and mounted, yet what Augustine remembered was not so much the success itself as the ambivalences of that success. But a close friend, perhaps the closest he ever had, was taken from him in a most disturbing way. (This friend, like the mother of his son, is left nameless.) The friend fell ill, and his family had the sacrament of baptism administered while he lay unconscious. The patient rallied, and Augustine, full of the optimistic ebullience of the moment, spoke slightingly of the ritual performed on the passive invalid. He was surprised to find that his friend took the sacrament seriously and brushed away Augustine's jibes. To make matters worse, the friend soon relapsed and died, in the peace of the church Augustine disdained. He had lost his friend to death, and to the church as well.

Episodes such as this make up the fragments of autobiography that occur in the second through fifth books of the *Confessions.* The tale of lapse and descent is not overdrawn, except that to those who do not share Augustine's harsh judgment on his younger self it may seem excessive to have assigned any moral significance at all to the ordinary anxieties and strains of life. The insistent pull of fleshly concupiscence, the inanities of philosophical speculation, and the impatience of ambition all conspired to make Augustine successful and dissatisfied; so far, Augustine is no different from many others before and since. The young Augustine, much as we seek to know him, eludes our grasp, as he escaped even the Augustine who wrote these pages.

This represented decline ends with the depiction Augustine gives of himself as he turned an uncertain corner to his thirtieth year. His Manicheism had left him, with his philosophical allegiance tentatively placed in the moribund school of academic skepticism, which still offered rationalism but was not embarrassed—as Manicheism was—by a body of idiosyncratic doctrines. Outwardly, the good of his career demanded that he make no break with the ruling orthodoxy. The dismal fifth book of the *Confessions* ends with the young Augustine betwixt and between, on the doorstep of the church, confused and doubting whether to enter:

> So then after the manner of the Academics (as they are supposed) doubting of every thing, and wavering between all, I settled so far, that the Manichees were to be abandoned;

judging that, even while doubting, I might not continue in that sect, to which I already preferred some of the philosophers;

to which philosophers notwithstanding, for that they were without the saving name of Christ, I utterly refused to commit the cure of my sick soul.

I determined therefore so long to be a catechumen of the Catholic Church, to which I had been commended by my parents, till something certain should dawn upon me, whither I might steer my course. (5.14.25)

Grace

Nothing so astonished Augustine as the change that came over him during his short years in Milan. For that divine gift—such he had to believe it—he reserved the central books of his *Confessions* of praise. To admire the majesty of the heavens or the workings of divine providence through human history is one thing. That detached, objective contemplation can be cheap and inconsequential. But when Augustine looked back on his own life, he was amazed at the evidences of growth and change. Seeing God at work in his own life, he would not deny the call that had made him a bishop.

No subject in the life of Augustine has excited so much discussion as the conversion he recounts in the *Confessions*. The reader facing those pages for the first time should be advised of some of the controversies and the importance that attaches to them.[6]

The bluntest question is the historian's: Is Augustine telling the truth? Does the highly selective, theological narrative of the *Confesssions* faithfully represent his life at that period, or has he taken liberties with the facts? He would later (in Book 10) expatiate at length on the peculiarities of memory: was he not perhaps himself the victim of memory's selective powers in this case? The first works written after the crucial events (mainly the Cassiciacum dialogues) do not support the narrative of the *Confessions* in abundant detail. If the garden scene of the Book 8 was so crucial to his whole life, why does no trace of it appear in any of the early works, some written as soon as three months after the event?

Broader questions deal not with the events themselves but with their significance. Augustine's reading of the writings of certain Platonists were instrumental in effecting his conversion to Christianity. How important a part did they play? Perhaps the events of 386 amounted not to a conversion to Christianity at all, but to a conversion to Neoplatonism. On that view, only Augustine's conscription into church affairs pulled him the distance further that made him a real Christian.

Scholars still divide over the questions of historicity and have clustered around an ambivalent answer concerning the influence of Neoplatonism. It is generally accepted that Augustine converted to Christianity in 386, but then it is also generally accepted that the Christianity of his early period was heavily laden with Neoplatonic ideas and expectations.

The disparities between the *Confessions* narrative and the Cassiciacum dialogues need not be significant, first of all, and can be explained by attending to the differences of literary style and purpose between those works. The dialogues were philosophical works in a Ciceronian mold, in which personal passions fit uncomfortably. The very proximity of the dialogues to the events of the conversion explains their reticence. (The dialogues were dedicated to some of his Milan friends; but it was just those friends to whom Augustine regrets having given a disingenuous explanation for his retirement: 9.2.2–4.) Having converted to a religion of humility and self-effacement, Augustine would not have trumpeted his inmost feelings so soon and in so self-serving a way. A full decade had to pass before he could devise the literary means, in the *Confessions,* to speak of his most private experiences without pose or brag.

The philosophical quality of the dialogues illuminates Augustine's relation to Neoplatonism. In 386 and immediately after, Augustine was a Christian convert but not yet a Christian theologian. Inexperience and the lack of relevant training held him back. Instead, he was a professor of Latin letters with some competence in philosophical analysis. He could write of the problems that Christianity raised within the strict technical competence of his professional experience. The context of these dialogues is more Ciceronian than Neoplatonic, and there is no lack at all of explicit references to Christianity; but the characteristic Augustinian method of argument, in widening exegetical circles starting from particular texts of scripture, is not yet there and only comes to full maturity about the time of Augustine's consecration as bishop.

Furthermore, no religious conversion is complete and instantaneous. The one who comes to a new creed always brings confused expectations and misunderstandings bred in another environment. From earliest manhood, Augustine had been looking for an answer to all life's questions, expecting a decisive turning by which every-

thing would be changed for the better. When he did finally turn
to Christianity, he seems to have had expectations the new religion
could not fulfill. (He seems, for example, to have been conditioned
to seek and expect what we could roughly call mystical visions; the
expectation is encouraged by Neoplatonism, but fades as Augustine
learns the Christian way of life.[7]) Perfect peace, serenity, and tran-
quility of spirit did not come automatically and permanently. In
the ten years between the conversion and the writing of the *Confessions,* Augustine modified his expectations and in doing so discovered
more accurately than he could have done before what was essential
about his new religion. Neoplatonic influences were at work in the
years after 386, but these influences were constantly on the wane,
for Augustine had taken Christianity as the new norm according to
which all other religious and philosophical notions were to be judged.[8]

In the central books of the *Confessions* (Books 6–9), Augustine
contemplates the events that led him to his new life. Much has been
selected, edited, and rearranged to make this picture. The description Augustine gives of these crucial events in his life is meant to
be theologically and spiritually accurate, arranged according to principles other than those of strict chronology. With that caution in
mind, the pattern and truth of these books become evident.

The patron of Augustine's turn to Christianity would seem to
have been Ambrose, whose sermons demolished intellectual barriers
Augustine had not been able to surmount for himself and whose
hands administered the baptism that made Augustine a member of
Christ's church. But Ambrose was always a little too high up and
far away for Augustine. The high affairs of the imperial court preoccupied Ambrose, and another ambitious courtier working his way
up into the fringes of that court cannot long have detained his
attention. He had seen many like Augustine before.

But Augustine may have emphasized Ambrose's remoteness to
contrast him with the Manichean leader Faustus in Book 5. He did
manage a private audience on at least one occasion (*Letters* 54.2.3).
He had sought Faustus's advice as of a guru, but found only some
oratorical skill, and Faustus wound up studying classical literature
under Augustine. He went to hear Ambrose, to observe his oratorical
style, was inspired to seek him out as a guru, but was rebuffed by
various difficulties. The Christian religion, we are meant to infer,
is not transmitted as secret doctrine by gurus, but proclaimed publicly from the pulpit for all. Augustine could never reach Ambrose

the guru, but Ambrose the bishop reached him with his words and baptised him with his hands.

Before that baptism, there was still a world of confusion and uncertainty to face.

And lo, I was now in my thirtieth year, sticking in the same mire, greedy of enjoying things present, which passed away and wasted my soul, while I said to myself, 'Tomorrow I shall find it. It will appear manifestly, and I shall grasp it. Lo, Faustus the Manichee will come and clear every thing! O you great men, ye Academicians, it is true then, that no certainty can be attained for the ordering of life? Nay, let us search the more diligently and despair not. Lo, things in the ecclesiastical books are not absurd to us now, which sometimes seemed absurd, and may be taken otherwise, and in a good sense. I will take my stand where as a child my parents placed me, until the clear truth be found out. But where shall it be sought or when? Ambrose has no leisure. We have no leisure to read. Where shall we find even the books? Whence, or when procure them? From whom borrow them? Let set times be appointed, and certain hours be ordered for the health of our soul. Great hope has dawned: the catholic faith teaches not what we thought, and vainly accused it of. Her instructed members hold it profane to believe God to be bounded by the figure of a human body. And do we doubt to *knock,* that the rest *may be opened?* The forenoons our scholars take up: what do we do during the rest of the day? Why not this? But when shall we pay court to our great friends, whose favor we need? When shall we compose what we may sell to scholars? When shall we refresh ourselves, unbending our minds from these intense cares?' (6.11.18)

Two problems continued to plague Augustine and suspend his assent to Christianity. The first he alluded to in the passage just quoted, and was twofold. First, there was the resolute materiality of the world we perceive and the consequent difficulty imagining any kind of existence not bound to visible, tangible forms. But then there was the gross corporeality of the Christian scriptures, particularly the Old Testament documents. Augustine was bound in a world-as-it-seemed and a view of Christianity that seemed no less bound to such a world.

Here Ambrose made from the pulpit his first contribution to Augustine's search. In his sermons, he showed Augustine for the first time Christian scriptural interpretation as Augustine would later describe it in *Christian Doctrine.* He elucidated the notion of spiritual being in a way that taught Augustine how to think of God without binding God to the world of matter. God as creator is only possible with such a vision. This finally undermined Augustine's Manicheism, which had labored to find a place in the material world for both God and evil. For Augustine, God had finally been liberated from the struggle with evil, and evil itself no longer needed to be given a material form.

Now the problem of evil itself could be faced in a context that gave promise of a solution. To judge by the arrangement of the *Confessions,* Augustine seems to say that the first advance in understanding occurred in 384 and early 385, shortly after his arrival in Milan, and there is verisimilitude to this. The initial impact of Ambrose on a mind like Augustine's should have been great. If that is true, then the second stage of Augustine's development, the resolution of the problem of evil, ran through the rest of 385 and perhaps into 386. For this, Ambrose was again, in a roundabout way, influential.

There was a lively interest in Ambrose's Milan in the writings of the late Platonists.[9] Even though one of the leading Platonic writers, Porphyry (died c. 305), had written a book directed against the Christians so vehement and effective that it was later the victim of an unusually successful book-burning campaign, many of the ideas of the Platonists were well-received. Marius Victorinus, of whom we shall hear again in closer connection with Augustine's conversion, had translated Greek Platonic writings into Latin, and these were widely read and discussed in the circle of intellectuals around Ambrose.[10]

Not unlike the scholastics of the later middle ages, these Christian Platonists used a secular philosophy to illuminate their own theological reflections. In the terms Augustine used in *Christian Doctrine,* they were spoiling the Egyptians of their gold. In an age when the trinitarian definitions of the Nicene creed were new-minted, Platonic discussions of the three hypostases (the One, the Mind, and the Spirit) sounded eerily similar to the Christian principles.[11] The vocabulary of the Platonists offered clarification for the complex and confusing testimony of scripture. Augustine was not a leader in this movement, but he was an eager learner. Just what he read and how he interpreted it remains a matter of heated controversy, but we can sketch his development with the help of the *Confessions.*

Augustine had been troubled all his adult life by the problem of evil. If God is all-good, the old question goes, how does evil arise?

Worse, if God created all things, does this not mean that he created evil itself? Is not a Manichean solution preferable to this blasphemy? The answer to which the Platonists led Augustine lay in the nature of being itself. Being is not, for the Platonists, something absolute, but something contingent. Material creation is not fully existent, but only participates in the being of the One, the creator (which the Christians would readily identify with God the Father). The One has perfect existence, but all other entities are only shadows of the ultimate model. Now all things are good insofar as they are created, that is, insofar as they participate in the being of God, but they are less than perfectly good insofar as they fail to resemble the all-good essence of God. The will of a rational creature is capable of turning toward God, hence participating more fully in God's goodness, and capable of turning away, hence participating less fully. Evil lies in the absence of good, in the willful separation from God that is the act of created beings. The natural tendency of created beings is to return to unity with God, to full goodness. Evil is merely the name given to the turning away from God of those beings. Properly speaking, evil inheres only in the wills of free, rational creatures. The other things men call evil (the violent deaths of innocent people in natural catastrophes, for example) are only manifestations of a divine providence that men, with an incomplete view of reality, cannot fathom. Suffering is punishment or trial for creatures, but is intrinsically good in itself insofar as it succeeds in reforming or purifying them. If it fails the failure is that of the creatures, not of God.

This is a stark and radical theodicy, by which all the evil of the world is taken on the shoulders of mankind. This principle would eventually smooth the way to Augustine's doctrine of original sin, an awesome doctrine, bearable only because it brings with it (for the believer) the hope the whole burden of evil does not stay with man, but has been asssumed again voluntarily by God, in the redeeming sacrifice of the cross.

Augustine's debt to Platonism is made explicit in the passage where he uses the first verses of the Gospel according to John as his touchstone for assessing the Platonic achievement (7.9.13–14). He finds in their writings plenty to parallel the notion of the preexistent Word and its function in creation, but what he finds lacking in them is anything to correspond to the fourteenth verse: "And the Word was made flesh, and dwelt among us." In that gap lies the difference between the despairing forced cheerfulness of the Platonist and the hope of the Christian.

Once Augustine had seen his way past the problem of evil to a recognition of his own guilt, all should have been well. Already at the end of Book 7, the Platonists and their writings have sent him to the pages of Saint Paul and he sings the praises of the divine grace (7.21.27). The intellectual obstacles to his acceptance of Christianity had fallen away. He may even at the time have thought that he had reached his goal (cf. 7.20.26: "I chattered on [about these matters] just like an expert.").

But Augustine was about to discover the last secret Christianity has in store for men of intellect and curiosity who consider its claims. In the end, intellect and curiosity are not enough. The mind may be satisfied, but there is more to Christianity than the intellectual apprehension of propositions; there is more to faith than belief. This discovery led Augustine to the final surrender of heart and will that he would later recognize as conversion.

The eighth book of the *Confessions* narrates—or, more precisely, seems to narrate the last stages of Augustine's conversion, for on examination it becomes clear that we are not given a definite account of an orderly sequence of events. Rather, a variety of episodes, with a similar theme but no indications of date, are grouped together to depict the growing pressure Augustine felt in the last weeks or months before the decisive episode.

The book is a compilation of conversion stories. Augustine and Alypius appear at the end of a line that includes the desert monk Saint Anthony, two unnamed courtiers of Augustine's own time, and the learned and renowned Marius Victorinus. The sequence begins with Victorinus, and we should not think it mere coincidence. The story is told to Augustine by Simplicianus, Ambrose's destined successor as bishop of Milan and the closest ecclesiastical friend Augustine made in Milan. Simplicianus heard Augustine tell of his encounter with the books of the Platonists in Victorinus's translation and saw a chance to tell Augustine a story about a man very like Augustine himself (8.2.3–5).[12]

Victorinus was a distinguished student and practitioner of rhetoric and philosophy who had a statue erected in his honor in the Roman forum. But he had also found himself drawn to Christianity. He confided to his friend Simplicianus that he was in fact already a Christian, but Simplicianus replied, "I will not believe it, nor will

I rank you among Christians, until I see you in the church of Christ."
Victorinus, like many another high-minded dabbler in religion,
replied with depreciating humor, "So is it walls that make people
Christian?" Simplicianus was unmoved, on that occasion and others,
and insisted on public affiliation, with eventual success.

Simplicianus's tale of Victorinus was doubtless meant to nag at
the professsor's spirit while he went on living in Milan, pursuing
his public activities as teacher, finding his attention brought again
and again to the startling tales of conversions that upset the routine
of life lived in the secular world. The courtiers who abandoned their
careers when they found a copy of the *Life of Saint Anthony* (by the
great Alexandrian bishop Athanasius) even showed him, all unsus-
pecting, the method of his decision. Beyond the public, civil Christian life in polite society, he began to encounter the monastic life,
outwardly shabby and unsocial, but increasingly attractive to many.
Anthony had shown the way for a radical renunciation of the secular
world that would challenge thoughtful Christians henceforth, whether
they actually left the secular world or not, to examine carefully the
conditions of secular life and see how far those conditions might be
compatible with Christian commitment.

The pressures mounted. The *Confessions* capture and analyze the
two-mindedness Augustine found in himself, conscious of two conflicting wills working within him simultaneously. His whole intellectual search had been an effort to reach a placid and measured
conclusion on the basis of which to effect a rational reorganization
of his life, but faith, that esssential turning of the will toward God,
is finally mysterious to the very people who live with it.

In later years Augustine would resist all efforts to resolve the
paradoxes of grace and will. He had good intellectual and spiritual
basis for that resistance, but the emotional hardihood that kept him
to his position in the face of all the pressures either to abandon his
definitions or to explain them in a facile way (and thus lapse either
into Pelagianism or Calvinism) came from his own experience. He
could not account for the turnings of his own will, much less for
those of anyone else. He knew that it was his will, that his decisions
were free and voluntary, but he also felt that those decisions were
fundamentally impotent ones. Another power had been working at
another level of his soul, and in the presence of that power the
ditherings of his own paltry liberty of choice were insignificant.

So the history of human salvation is the history of human will and effort leading to sin and error counterbalanced by divine will overmastering human powers and leading people back to knowledge and holiness. Because the process affects the very foundations of knowing and willing, it is impossible to represent it fairly in human language. Those who have known the experience can never fully or adequately represent it to those who have not. Augustine's example shows us that even the most sensitive of converts finds it difficult to reconstruct the situation in which it was possible not to be a believer, and this only makes it harder for the outsider to find the picture credible. Rational argument may go on, and the hidden workings of grace may use those arguments as instruments, but the main business of Christianity is not subject to human control or management.

> Thus soul-sick was I, and tormented,
> accusing myself much more severely than my wont,
> rolling and turning in my chains,
> till they were wholly broken,
> whereby I now was barely held, but still was held.
> . . . For I said within myself,
> 'Be it done now, be it done now.'
> And as I spake, I all but enacted it.
> I all but did it, and did it not;
> yet I sank not back to my former state,
> but kept my stand hard by, and took breath.
> . . . The very toys of toys, and vanities of vanities,
> my ancient mistresses, still held me;
> they plucked my fleshly garment, and whispered softly,
> 'Dost thou cast us off? and from that moment
> shall we no more be with thee for ever?'
>   (8.11.25–26)

The climactic scene that follows in the garden at Milan is unobtrusively surrounded with echoes of other moments. The fig tree that will appear, for example, may very well have stood in that garden, but we cannot notice it without recalling another fig tree in the gospel (Jn. 1.48–50). Once again we are drawn to consider the questions of historicity raised by this account, but if we are prudent we will dismiss them as irrelevant. The personal authenticity of what Augustine recounts to us makes his reliability as an

observer of surrounding events at the moment of secondary importance. Whether it happened this way or not (to an outside observer's
judgment), it is perfectly clear that this is the way it was lived,
and that is all that matters.

Augustine was sitting with Alypius in a private garden. "But
when a deep consideration had from the secret bottom of my soul
drawn together and heaped up all my misery in the sight of my
heart, there arose a mighty storm, bringing a mighty shower of
tears" (8.12.28). (Early Christians lived closer than their modern
counterparts to the brink of tears in prayer, tears of compunction.)
Augustine goes apart from Alypius: "solitude was suggested to me
as fitter for the business of weeping."

I cast myself down, I know not how, under a fig-tree, giving full vent to
my tears; and the floods of mine eyes gushed out, an *acceptable sacrifice to
Thee.*
    And, not indeed in these words, yet to this end, I spake much unto
Thee: *"And Thou, O Lord, how long? How long, Lord, wilt thou be angry, for
ever? Remember not our past iniquities,"* for I felt I was held by them.
    So was I speaking, and weeping in the most bitter contrition of my
heart, when, lo!, I heard from a neighboring house a voice, as of a boy
or girl, I know not, chanting, and often repeating, "Take up, read; take
up, read." Instantly my countenance altered and I began to think most
intently, whether children were wont in any kind of play to sing such
words, nor could I remember ever to have heard the like. (8.12.29)

It has been suggested that the neighboring house was a church and
the words part of a liturgical ceremony; that the words were spoken
by real children; and that it was all a hallucination that Augustine
cheerfully read as a sign from heaven. But Augustine himself left
the question open. The curious psychological verisimilitude of a
situation in which his first thought was not to obey but to ask
pedantic questions about the source is worth noticing.

Augustine acted quickly enough, though. He remembered what
he had heard of Anthony, that a chance encounter with the words
of the Gospel had changed his life. So he went back to where Alypius
was sitting and took the copy of Paul they had been reading. He
fell upon the first words that came to his eye.

*"Not in rioting and drunkenness, not in chambering and wantonness, not in strife
and envying: but put ye on the Lord Jesus Christ, and make not provision for the*

flesh in concupiscence" (Rom. 13.13–14). No further would I read, nor did I need to: for instantly at the end of this sentence, by a light of serenity infused into my heart, all darkness of doubt fled away.

"We have no right and we should not have the presumption to say that when he rose from his knees in the Milan garden he was not altogether a 'new man.'"[13] Alypius, reading further on the same page of Paul, found a text for himself and joined Augustine's resolve. Augustine is hard on himself in Book 9 for having equivocated about the step he should take next. He determined to stay out the teaching term a few weeks longer rather than break away and resign immediately, and when he handed in his resignation he alleged weakness of health—true, but incomplete as an explanation. (However strong the effect of the garden scene immediately, only time could prove that it was not a false dawn.)

Shortly after began the country-house idyll at Cassiciacum. The habits of the intellect were too deeply ingrained to break suddenly, but we are also told that Augustine would lie awake half the night, praying with tears. In the *Confessions* Augustine offers here a reading of a Psalm text to show his new relationship with the scriptures. In the spring, the group came back to Milan and Augustine and Alypius were baptised—a further step also dismissed in a few lines. The scene in the garden was private; the baptism made the decision reached there public. Walls do not indeed make people Christian, but Augustine was only fully a Christian when he had entered those walls as a full member of the sacramental community. (In Augustine's time, the eucharistic ritual was a matter not discussed openly before the unbaptised; hence we are frustrated at having no testimony here of the impression that ritual, and the sense of participation that came with it, made, but the importance of the sacrament should not be ignored because of ignorance.)

The narrative is almost at an end at this point, but Augustine has one last debt to pay. In the short time Monica survived his baptism (less than a year), mother and son finally understood each other. Not long before death overtook her as their party waited at Ostia for a ship to Africa, an event occurred that seemed to Augustine to complete the transition he had begun.

Augustine knew better than to try to have a name for what happened at Ostia. He certainly knew better than to make it out to be more than it was. A foretaste of heaven, coming as it did just before his mother's death, had a particular symbolic force, but despite the parallels with Neoplatonic rapture, Augustine the bishop did not think the whole of the Christian life would be a succession of these dramatic moments.[14] What he was granted with his mother in those moments by another garden was just one more gift. The ecstasy of mysticism is one of the highest and greatest gifts, but it is inessential.

The whole chapter should be read to appreciate the quality of the moment (9.10.23–26). The sensible world fell away and mother and son were completely at sea in their shared union with God. This is in an important sense the decisive encounter with the Word of God that had been only adumbrated in all the previous moments depicted in the *Confessions,* even the one in that garden at Milan. This particular narrative comes, moreover, in a literary work that is itself of a mystical kind. The special qualities Augustine brings to this particular event are those of the time of his writing of the *Confessions.* Memory and accurate reportage alone could not make the moment come alive.

Monica's last message to her son as they stood together was to be a theme for the rest of the life he faced from then on. "Son, for my own part I have no further delight in any thing in this life." Her only worldly hope, for the conversion of her son, had been fulfilled. "My God hath done this for me more abundantly, that I should now see thee withal, despising earthly happiness, become his servant: what am I doing still here?" (9.10.26).

The saints are those who live in the world but who are not quite of it. If we are justified in calling Augustine a saint, it is probably accurate to say that he began to live his sainthood just at this moment. Henceforth, he knew a freedom he had only suspected might exist before. His future as a servant of God was out of his own hands. His immediate return to Africa and the foundation of the quasi-monastic community at Tagaste were to be thwarted by other needs of the church. He wound up in a city far from his cloister, far from all the ambitions he had known, perfectly content to do the work he found himself busied with. (Augustine in Hippo and Newman in Birmingham resemble each other in more than a few ways, not least in the misplaced pity of those who think their talents wasted in such obscurity.) The autobiography of Augustine the sinner is at an end. Henceforth, Augustine is freed of time and narrative, and his *Confessions* reflect that freedom.

Free Will

With Book 10, the reader must give up all hope of concluding
that the *Confessions* are autobiography in any conventional sense.
What narrative line there had been is lost altogether and a more
complex literary strategy obtrudes its presence upon the reader.
While it has been fashionable to argue whether the last four books
have anything to do with the first nine, the simple bulk of the
material should give us pause: two-fifths of the work's pages remain,
and scarcely an autobiographical scrap is to be found among them.
We might rather argue that, since the pieces of reminiscence are so
clearly confined to one part of the work, it is more remarkable that
the impression could ever have grown that the work was autobiography at all.

The place to begin to seek an authentic reading of this work is
still with the fact of prayer. The first nine books of the *Confessions,*
written by the neophyte bishop in his first episcopal years at Hippo,
present a double image to our consideration. They are about the
early life of a sinful young man determined to find his own way to
salvation but destined to be dragged off in a direction he at first
resented. But they are also the prayerful reflection on those events
of a mature man, a bishop in the church of Christ, living out the
transformation those books describe.

In Book 10 the images of the past fade away and we are left to
face Augustine the bishop, the product of the years of growth and
change the first books suggest to us. What we know of the early
Augustine comes to us in the main through the eyes of this middle-
aged man. Any reading of the *Confessions* that does not confront
him, and not merely the phantasms of the young Augustine that
he presents, is doomed to inadequacy. And this bishop is a man of
prayer.

But perhaps we need a more subtle description of the nature of
prayer and confession to understand what is going on here. Prayer
is endemic to the human condition, in all places and cultures. We
know full well how self-centered and unloving such prayer can be,
even when it is as innocent as the child's plea for a new toy or
revenge on a playmate. Prayer, the turning of the mind and heart
to God, takes place even where grace is absent, but this inferior
communication between God and man is still evidence of the possibility of authentic communication.[15]

The sinner who prays in ignorance and darkness prays badly, and prays in the imperative and subjunctive moods. He commands God to give him what he wants, he pleads his cause. God's will is of no account. Such prayer begins to become authentic only when it is founded in the knowledge that comes of revelation. God reaches down to mankind with the gospel, and this forms the basis for the transformation of the individual (we saw all this on the first page of the *Confessions*). Gradually, immature prayer becomes what we will call (to distinguish it from the immature variety and to conform to Augustine's usage) confession. The fully enlightened Christian would no long need to speak in the unreal grammar of imperative and subjunctive. What God has promised, God gives, and the indicative mood is adequate to present this. Hence, there is no longer need for plea and impetration, but for confession and acceptance.

Prayer of the second kind is what Augustine the bishop is seeking throughout the *Confessions*. Confession is man's part in revelation: God reveals, man praises, and the circle is complete. In mortal life the process is imperfect, but the only business of the saints in heaven is the praise of God, the complete fullness of confession begun here below in the dark light of revelation.

Augustine's literary *Confessions* fall then into two parts: there is the reassessment of his own past in the light of divine mercy that filled the first books. Augustine lived through those years under a variety of delusions about himself and the world; as bishop he can now look back in the light of revelation and see the true pattern of those years. What was, as it was lived through, a puzzling search for truth and knowledge, turns out to have been a piece of Christian salvation history all along, with its own fall into sin and rise through grace.

But Augustine in the *Confessions* was concerned with the present as much as with the past. Present imperfections were as puzzling and important to him as those of his past. Confession is difficult and its success only partial, for the author of the confession is still sinful and in need of grace lest he fall again. The last books of the *Confessions,* among other things, bring us to Augustine at the moment of confession. They present him, as he could then imagine himself, and they present his praise of God, working in him as he then saw it.

The structure he imparts to this confession resembles a conventional examination of conscience. To the outsider, such considerations can easily seem morbid and self-absorbed. Here again the outsider is at a disadvantage. The whole of the *Confessions* is a self-examination in the light of divine truth, and what passes for examination of conscience is only a small part of this whole.

On another level, Augustine is demolishing his own human words by the instrumentality of the divine Word. What were inadequate words arranged in immature prayer now become an embodiment of the Word itself being given back to God. The authority for all speech comes not from the human voice itself but from God's Word, wholly outside human comprehension. Human beings no longer comprehend themselves with their words, but God's word comprehends human beings and revitalizes all discourse. What men say has meaning only if the divine Word speaks through them. What men say of and for themselves is inauthentic. Prayer, in its fulfilled form as confession, is the only form of discourse with a claim to legitimacy. Confession becomes the vital basis of all discourse, hence of all human life insofar as it is human. ("Pray without ceasing": 1 Thess. 5.17.) All that is not confession is partial and imperfect by comparison.

> Let me know Thee, O Lord, who knowest me:
> *let me know Thee, as I am known.*
> Power of my soul,
> enter into it, and fit it for Thee,
> that Thou mayest have and hold it
> *without spot or wrinkle.*
> This is my hope, *therefore do I speak.*
>   (10.1.1)

The scriptural echoes are unusually important here. First, Augustine uses God's own words to make the central prayer of the whole work—for self-knowledge based in divine knowledge. Then he offers his whole soul to God as something to be possessed "without spot or wrinkle," deliberately using a phrase explicitly applied in scripture to the church as a whole (Eph. 5.27). The individual human soul is inextricably part of the church and hence resembles it. Finally, God's Word itself is the justification for speaking at all.

For behold, Thou *lovest the Truth,*
and *he that doth the truth,*
cometh to the light.
This would I do in my heart before Thee in confession,
and in my writing, before many witnesses.

God himself strictly does not need the literary artifact for the act
of confession to be complete, but the text is the instrument by
which confession comes before men as well as God and hence obeys
the twofold command to love neighbor as well as God. Putting
confession in writing does not limit or narrow its authenticity, but
completes it and makes it a part of the life of the whole church,
the instrument of God's redemption on earth.

What then have I to do with men,
that they should hear my confessions . . . ?
A race curious to know the lives of others,
slothful to amend their own.
Why seek they to hear from me what I am,
who will not hear from Thee what themselves are?
And how do they know whether I speak true,
when from myself they hear of myself,
seeing *no man knows what is in man*
but the spirit of man which is in him?

(10.3.3)

The question of credibility underlines the question of authenticity.
Why should readers who come to the work in detachment and
skepticism, merely curious to know what another isolated individual
happens to be like, believe what they read here? Will not skeptical
readers take this text prisoner, make it the grounds for their own
religious, historical, or psychoanalytical speculations, and ignore
the author and his message?

But because *charity believeth all things*
(that is, among those whom,
knitting them unto itself, it maketh one)
I also, O Lord, will in such wise confess unto Thee,
that men may hear,
to whom I cannot demonstrate whether I confess truly;
yet they believe me,
whose ears charity openeth unto me.

The answer lies in God's grace. Those who are bound together by
the love of God, and who are therefore part of the church, will see
and understand in his story their own stories. Salvation history is
always and everywhere the same, and Augustine's story is—insofar
as it is true confession in the special sense—the story of every soul
touched by grace. Charity, the substance of grace at work in the
world, becomes the means by which barriers of suspicion and detachment are eradicated, and readers come to share the experience
of a writer. This is not a book to be read so much as it is a prayer
in which the reader is to share.

But what I now am, at the very time of making these confessions, diverse
people desire to know, who have or have not known me, who have heard
from me or of me. But their ear is not at my heart, where I am, whatever
I am. They wish then to hear me confess what I am within, whither neither
their eye, nor ear, nor understanding, can reach. They wish it, as ready
to believe—but will they know? For charity, whereby they are good,
telleth them, that in my confessions I lie not; and she in them, believeth
me. . . . But for what fruit would they hear this? Do they desire to
rejoice with me, when they hear how near, by Thy gift, I approach unto
Thee? And to pray for me, when they shall hear how much I am held
back by my own weight? To such will I discover myself. (10.3.4–10.4.5)

And so the microscopic self-examination begins, at much less
distance than the voyage of memory in the early books had allowed
him to stand.

Yet I know something of Thee, which I know not of myself. Truly, now
we see *through a glass darkly,* not *face to face* as yet. So long therefore as I
be absent from Thee, I am more present with myself than with Thee; and
yet know I Thee that Thou art in no ways passible; but I, what temptations
I can resist, what I cannot, I know not. I will confess then what I know
of myself, I will confess also what I know not of myself. And that because
what I do know of myself, I know by Thy shining upon me; and what I
know not of myself, so long I know it not, until my darkness be made
as the noon-day in Thy countenance. (10.5.7)

Even now Augustine cannot escape from the fields of memory.
All human consciousness and existence find themselves, Augustine
discovers, in the memory, which is the foundation of identity. If
the chance agglomeration of sense experiences were all I possessed,

I would be lost in the void of the amnesiac. To begin to understand himself, Augustine must now try to understand the faculty that he has used with such success to recapture his early life. As he comes to the present, he discovers that a substantial part of what he is, and therefore of what he wants to represent to his God and to his brothers and sisters is that power of memory itself. That is what makes Augustine recognizably himself.

Great is the power of memory, a fearful thing, O my God, a deep and boundless manifoldness; and this thing is the mind, and this am I myself. What am I then, O my God? What nature am I? A life various and manifold, and exceeding immense. Behold the plains, and caves, and caverns of my memory, innumerable and innumerably full of innumerable things. (10.17.26)

Memory is where Augustine must be when he searches for God. In authentic self-knowledge, Augustine knows God.

See what a space I have gone over in my memory seeking Thee, O Lord; and I have not found Thee without it. . . . But where in my memory residest Thou, O Lord, where residest Thou there? What manner of lodging hast Thou framed for Thee? . . . I entered into the very seat of my mind (which it hath in my memory, inasmuch as the mind remembers also) neither wert Thou there. . . . Where then did I find Thee, that I might learn Thee, but in Thee above me? Place there is none. . . . Everywhere, O truth, dost Thou give audience to all who ask counsel of Thee, and at once answerest all. (10.24.35)

The self itself, seat of all human identity, is not absolute but contingent. We do not find God in the self as much as we find that the self is in God. With this secret of self-knowledge finally revealed, Augustine is ready to see himself as he is.

Augustine's ensuing meditations on his moral state as bishop are alien to us. If the revelations of the first books seem a little tame to the sensation-seeker, the content of Book 10 seems downright neurotic. Here is a man who has meditated long and hard on the will of God and the power of grace, devoting himself in mature years to niggling criticism of his own habits and actions. What, for example, is a bishop doing deploring church music?

For at times he wishes the whole melody of sweet music used to accompany the Psalter could be banished from his ears and his church's too. "That mode seems to me safer, which I remember to have been told often of Athanasius, Bishop of Alexandria, who made the reader of the Psalm utter it with so slight inflection that it was nearer speaking than singing. . . . Yet when it befalls me to be more moved with the voice than the words sung, I confess to have sinned penally, and then had rather not hear music" (10.33.49–50).

There is more than absurd scrupulosity at work here. As bishop of a Christian church, living in monastic simplicity in plain sight of a large community, Augustine was all but immune to the greater faults of life that flesh is heir to. The natural result of this state is complacency, a confidence that one has finally triumphed over sin because one has finally triumphed over the obvious forms of sin. No such comfort is to Augustine's taste. Just as he can see the gratuitous love of wrong in his theft of pears at age sixteen, so now he knows that, even for a bishop, at every turn, the things of this world hold a perilous attraction for the soul, tying it down and keeping it from its natural course of ascent to God.

Even to phrase the issue that way is to misrepresent it to Augustine's disadvantage. Better to say that the fallen will turns towards the things of the world more than is their due, misdirecting their use towards self-enjoyment rather than the love of God. The ensuing enshacklement is, like all sin, entirely self-inflicted. The things of this world are not at fault for being beautiful, but even things of this world explicitly in the service of God, like the melodies of church music, are no less an opportunity for error than the more obvious temptations.

This scrupulous analysis of the attraction inherent in material things may seem to spring from a world-denying attitude, a painful and extreme puritanism. But this view is only possible if Augustine's main point is ignored. To affirm the world to the exclusion of God does harm, not only to the individual, but to the world itself. To make an idol of something or someone is dangerous no less to the idol than to the idolator. Augustine is so confident of the persistent power of the world to exercise its attraction, that he feels safe in counterbalancing that power with his own deep suspicion.

Notwithstanding, in how many most petty and contemptible things is our curiosity daily tempted, and how often we give way, who can recount? . . . I go not now to the circus to see a dog coursing a hare; but in the field, if passing, that coursing peradventure will distract me even from some weighty thought, and draw me after it: not that I turn aside the body of my beast, yet still incline my mind thither. (10.35.57)

Even though he quickly turns such distractions to profit in the contemplation of God's works, he is still dissatisfied: "To rise quickly is one thing, but it is another matter not to fall."

In this attitude lies a strain of perfectionism that is not necessarily morbid. Augustine refuses to be satisfied with himself as imperfect creature; but at the same time, by his very act of confession, we see that he recognizes and acknowledges the imperfections he shuns. He knows full well that complete perfection is not a gift granted in this life. Compunction in its absence is a high gift and in itself a sign of the growing attraction to the heavenly life. To go on, aware of imperfections, however trivial, is a better thing than to make light of them. Augustine's horror at the moral evil in the world around him is genuine; if it were not matched by comparable horror at the evil and possibility of evil within, it would scarcely be sincere.

And Thou knowest how far Thou hast already changed me, who first healed me of the lust of vindicating myself, that Thou might forgive all the rest of my iniquities, and heal my infirmities, and redeem my life from corruption, and crown me with mercy and pity, and satisfy my desire with good things. . . . But, O Lord, . . . hath this third kind of temptation also ceased from me, or can it cease through this whole life? To wish, namely, to be feared and loved of men, for no other end, but that we may have a joy which is no joy. (10.36.58)

The final trap that awaits Augustine the bishop is the one that would suggest to him that he is now, after all, a bishop; he has, after all, put his whole life on paper for the world to see. Now, surely, at last, he is able to grasp the reins of power and become the great man, God's special messenger, that he was always meant to be. The respect and admiration of his flock strengthen a sense of separateness and importance, while the hostility of heretics and others outside can underline a tendency to self-righteousness. Bishops so closely resemble worldly governors that they are readily assumed to live according to the same principles of power and personal aggrandizement. That assumption itself puts great pressure on the occupants of the office, however strong their intention to remain untouched by the temptations.

The self-portrait of Augustine in his weaknesses comes to an end. His past is a story of personal inadequacy redeemed by divine mystery, his present is a continuing story of subjection to all the temptations the fallen will finds in the world, but his case is not hopeless. Grace has taken a hand in his life, and the chasm separating him from God is neither infinite nor incapable of being bridged. Here the story of the first ten books come full circle. On the first page of the *Confessions,* it was God who intervened to make all discourse possible, through Christ's preaching ministry. Now at the end of the tenth book, God's intervention again is necessary to make the speaker himself whole and healthy, this time through Christ's redemptive mystery.

But the true Mediator, whom in Thy secret mercy Thou hast showed to the humble, and sent, that by his example also they might learn that same humility, that *Mediator between God and man, the man Christ Jesus,* appeared between mortal sinners and the immortal just one; mortal with men, just with God. (10.43.68)

Christ is both victor and victim, both priest and sacrifice, the Word made flesh and dwelling among men.

Affrighted with my sins and the burden of my misery, I had cast in my heart, and had purposed to *flee to the wilderness;* but Thou forbade me, and strengthened me, saying *Therefore Christ died for all, that they which live may now no longer live unto themselves but unto Him that died for them.* (10.43.70)

Augustine's memoirs lead up to this page of the *Confessions,* with its act of faith. The turn to God that faith entails is constant and unceasing. Each hour brings a new conversion, from past sins to future hope, leaving behind the self bound in time and mortality to contemplate the transforming power of God outside all time and creation. Augustine's mission as bishop is to turn his back on the past and live only for, not the future, but the present—conceived as eternal. In Book 11 he is compelled to consider time itself as evidence of the created nature of earthly things, but for now, Augustine has come to the end of his past, escaping from time into history, leaving himself behind and embracing the Christ who gives history meaning.

Too late I loved Thee,
O Thou Beauty of ancient days, yet ever new!
too late I loved Thee!
And behold, Thou wert within, and I abroad,
and there I searched for Thee;
deformed I, plunging amid those fair forms,
which Thou hast made.
Thou wert with me, but I was not with Thee.
Things held me far from Thee,
which, unless they were in Thee, were not at all.
Thou called, and shouted, and burst my deafness.
Thou flashed, shone, and scattered my blindness.
Thou breathed odors, and *I drew in breath*
and *I sigh for Thee.*
I tasted, and *hunger and thirst.*
Thou touched me, and I burned for Thy peace.

(10.27.38)

In the Image and Likeness of God

The last three books of the *Confessions* are the principal obstacle
to the work's reputation for greatsess in the literary, as well as the
psychological or theological, order. One scholar recounted no less
than nineteen different theories that had been devised to explain
their presence and their relation to the rest of the work, then proceeded to add his own.[17] Consensus still eludes us. What follows
is neither a majority view (for there is none) nor simple idiosyncrasy,
but the serious student should bear in mind that different interpretations abound.

The first ten books of the *Confesssions* move from the origins of
fallen life to the dynamic present of the author, writing c. 397.
The first page of the work states the conditions out of which all
reasonable speech arises and the first book takes us back to the
author's infancy. In the books that follow, the narrative takes the
author from a state of original sin to a state of sacramental grace.
The text proceeds from the origins of all discourse in divine revelation to the fulfillment of discourse in the redemption effected by
the incarnate Word. So far goes salvation history, down to the
present, in both the structure and content of the narrative.

What can possibly be left? The answer is trite but newly illuminating: God and the soul. *Noverim me, noverim te* is still an adequate

summary of Augustine's aspirations. But now the fundamental rupture separating creature and creator has been healed. History is over, in that sense. A bond of unity has been reforged. The future is now no longer the story of sin in the world of time but of love in the world of timelessness. The Christian lives in time betweeen history and eternity, and it is into that world that Augustine the author now escapes.

Book 11 opens in this new, divine present. Augustine now sees himself standing in time, facing the eternal divinity: "Lord, since eternity is Thine, art Thou ignorant of what I say to Thee?" (11.1.1).

But how shall I suffice with the tongue of my pen to utter all Thy exhortations, and all Thy terrors, and comforts, and guidances, whereby Thou broughtest me to preach Thy word, and dispense Thy Sacrament to Thy people? And if I suffice to utter them in order, the drops of time are precious with me. Long have I burned to *meditate in Thy law,* and therein to confess to Thee my skill and unskillfulness, the daybreak of Thy enlightening, and the remnants of my darkness, until infirmity be swallowed up by strength. And I would not have aught besides steal away those hours which I find free from the necessities of refreshing my body and the powers of my mind, and from the service which we owe to men, or which though we owe not, yet we pay. (11.2.2)

At the end of his journey through memory in the praise of God, Augustine finds himself left with the scriptural text itself, the visible form of the divine revelation, through which to perform his sacrifice of praise and prayer. The study of scripture in this sense is not a special task set upon him because he is a bishop of the Christian church, for the last sentence makes clear that the duties of his office tend to impede his devotion rather than to enhance it. The duty to preach God's Word imposes responsibilities that could take Augustine further and further from his own personal encounter with that Word. Public responsibility and private need should coincide, but in a fallen world such is not always the case.

> Lord, my God, give ear unto my prayer,
> and let Thy mercy hearken unto my desire:
> because it is anxious not for myself alone,
> but would serve brotherly charity.
> . . . Grant thereof a space for our meditations
> in the *hidden things of Thy law,*

and close it not against us *who knock.*
For not in vain wouldst Thou have the darksome secrets
of so many pages written:
nor are those forests without their harts
which retire therein and range and walk,
feed, lie down, and ruminate.
. . . Let me confess unto Thee
whatsoever I shall find in Thy books,
and *hear the voice of praise,*
and drink in Thee,
and meditate on the *wonderful things of Thy law;*
even from *the beginning,*
wherein *Thou madest the heaven and the earth,*
unto the everlasting reign of Thy holy city with Thee.
(11.2.3)

The circle is full. The Word of God inspires quest and praise to begin, and the fullness of that quest in this life is a return to the words of God in scripture. We have here a preview of the content of the last three books: they will explicate the Genesis account of creation, in which the whole history of creation is summed up. (The seventh day of creation is the day of eternal rest towards which the holy city proceeds; the first six days represent, *inter alia,* the six ages of man.) The last three books are thus an emblem of all scriptural study, since they treat in detail a passage of scripture that stands for the whole.

The opening chapters of Genesis were a constant source of illumination for Augustine; in the years just following the writing of the *Confessions* he would write his great *Literal Commentary on Genesis.* These last three books of *Confessions* give only a highly selective sketch of Augustine's ideas on the subjects raised. They bear looking into, to see what else is going on besides the simple exposition of a few verses of ancient Jewish scripture. We find in them not merely an exposition of scripture, but a self-conscious exposition of exposition itself. The principles of *Christian Doctrine* should be kept steadily in mind while we examine these pages written so shortly after.

The core of Christian doctrine is contained in the first line of Genesis: "In the beginning, God created heaven and earth, and the spirit of God was over the waters." The fathers saw allusion here to all three persons of the trinity. The words "in the beginning" are the same as those that begin John's Gospel: "In the beginning was the Word," which all Christians took to denote the second person of the trinity. Since even Augustine would know that the Greek version of the phrase could indicate not merely circumstance but even instrument ("by means of the beginning"), it was easy to assume that the deeper sense of the opening line revealed the three persons of the trinity were actively present in the act of creation from the outset.

Any creation narrative implies a doctrine about the nature of God and the nature of creature, focused on the process of creation itself. Augustine sees this, but almost immediately diverts his discussion into what often looks to readers like a digression, the long discussion of time that fills Book 11. He introduces the subject with the only joke in the *Confessions*:

See, I answer him that asketh, 'What did God do before He made heaven and earth?' I answer not as one is said to have done merrily (eluding the point of the question), 'he was preparing hell (saith he) for pryers into mysteries.' (11.12.14)

Augustine will answer the question seriously, for in it lies not merely the abstract subject of time but the essence of creature, creator, and creation, joined together in a unique philosophical nexus. The bulk of Book 11 works out a long and complex inquiry into the nature of time. Philosophers still read these pages with curiosity and interest.[18] For our immediate purposes, it is sufficient to consider the conclusion he reaches.

It is in thee, my mind, that I measure times. . . . The impression, which things as they pass by cause in thee, remains even when they are gone. This which is still present, I measure, not the things which pass by to make this impression. This I measure, when I measure times. Either then this is time, or I do not measure times. (11.27.36)

Time is inherent in the created intellect, a category for describing the apparent transience and impermanence of reality. Time is not even a created thing, for it is a creation of created things. Intelligent created beings see the world around themselves in a framework of their own invention, which they call time. This characteristic distinguishes their experience from that of their creator. God as creator sees all things simultaneously in a single vision, perceiving process and change but, freed of experiencing those things in temporal succession, he does not experience time. The creator lives outside created things and therefore, a fortiori, outside time. Time cannot be, Augustine concludes, without created being.

Book 11, therefore, seems to deal with the fact of creation in the scriptural text and the problem of time as theological obstacle. But these two tasks are one and the same. The book is thus in reality devoted to the question of creation itself, looking at all times to the first person of the trinity, God the Father of all things, eternal being who creates all contingent, temporal being. Book 11 is therefore the book of creation.

Book 12 is by contrast the book of God's words; that is, of scripture; that is, of knowledge—for all authentic knowledge comes from divine revelation. The formal pretext for the discussion of Book 12 is the distinction between heaven and earth, which Augustine takes allegorically to represent the differences between spirit and matter—between things as they are and things as they seem. God's knowledge, manifested to us, reveals this distinction. Otherwise we would be caught forever in the world of appearances.

Wondrous depth of Thy words! whose surface, behold! is before us, inviting to little ones. Yet are they a wondrous depth, O my God, a wondrous depth! It is aweful to look therein, an awefulness of honour and a trembling of love. (12.14.17)

Revelation is ambivalent and multi-leveled. The enhancement of human knowledge is thus a constant transition from surface knowledge to inner knowledge, from letter to spirit, from material appearances to spiritual, inner reality.

Just as Book 11 contained a long exploration of the problem of time itself, with full consideration of objections and alternatives, so too the matter of Book 12 is elucidated in an imagined debate with those who would gainsay the Christian interpretation of scripture.

With these words I now parley a little in Thy presence, O my God, who grant all these things to be true, which Thy truth whispers unto my soul. For those who deny these things, let them bark and deafen themselves as much as they please. I will essay to persuade them to quiet, and to open

118   AUGUSTINE

in them a way for Thy Word. But if they refuse, and repel me, I beseech,
O my God, *be not Thou silent to me.* (12.16.23)

The apparent movement of reading is from text to author, from
message to intention, but revelation short—circuits the process.
Something beyond mortal grasp intrudes to keep the reader from
moving directly from the written word to the intention of the human
author.

For behold, O my God, I Thy servant, who have in this book vowed a
sacrifice of confession unto Thee, and who pray, that by Thy mercy *I may
pay my vows unto Thee,* can I, with the same confidence wherewith I affirm,
that in Thy incommutable world Thou createdst all things visible and
invisible, affirm also, that Moses meant no other than this, when he wrote,
In the beginning God made heaven and earth? No. Because I see not in his
mind, that he thought of this when he wrote these things, as I do see it
in Thy truth to be certain. For he might have his thoughts upon God's
commencement of creating, when he said *In the beginning,* and by *heaven
and earth,* in this place he might intend no formed and perfected nature
whether spiritual or corporeal, but both of them inchoate and as yet
formless. For I perceive that whichsoever of the two had been said, it
might have been truly said; but which of the two he thought of in these
words, I do not so perceive. Although, whether it were either of these,
or any sense beside that I have not here mentioned, which this so great
man saw in his mind, when he uttered these words, I doubt not but that
he saw it truly, and expressed it aptly. (12.24.33)

The business of language is enlightenment, but in human hands
it leads to uncertainty and confusion. But revelation, working in
the hearts of believers and in the church as a whole, communicates
through written texts that spring from human minds and circum-
vents the sequence of author-intention-text. The author is no longer
a mythic icon established by the reader in accord with his reading
of the text, nor is the text so established either. Instead, both are
reduced to instruments through which a deeper truth about God
and hence man can be descried. We know when we have used the
text properly not from any self-verifying quality of the text itself,
but because the independent act of God authorizes the text through
the church externally and through faith internally. The only word,
in other words, is the Word.

If this is a fair summary of the content of Book 12 of the *Confessions,*
a pattern is forming. Book 11 dealt with existence, both temporal

and eternal, and led to God as creator and to the creature's relation to that God. Book 12 dealt with the conditions of knowledge, elucidating the nature of knowledge through the revelation of the Word of God in the hearts of believers. If this pattern continues, we should expect to find in the thirteenth book some indication of the presence of the third person of the trinity. [19]

And in fact the full trinity is the subject of the opening pages of Book 13, and with that discussion comes the clue we need to see the pattern for the last books. The three fundamental qualities of existent being, Augustine says (13.11.12), are existence, knowledge, and will. We have encountered this trinity before in the human personality; now we see it deriving from the godhead itself. God the Father is God as eternal being, source of all that exists; God the Son is God as knowledge, source of all that knows and is known; and God the Spirit is God as will, that is to say, God as love, source of all motion of heart and spirit.

With the fullness of trinitarian doctrine as it is imagined in Book 13, unity and variety, the many and the one, have been harmonized in a system of unusual durability and stability. But Augustine is not content merely to imagine the reality in a void. The thirteenth book shows the spirit alive in the world and hence completes the triad begun in Book 11.

The presence of the Spirit in the world is the church: Pentecost proclaimed as much. Hence Augustine turns to consider the sacraments, the deeds of the spirit through the church in the world. (Scriptural language begins to predominate more and more in this book. We near the end in the presence of the spirit.) Consider the paragraph, for example, beginning with the imagined command to baptism: "But first, wash you, be clean. . ." (13.19.24). Augustine's own baptism was a high point of Book 9, the culmination of his conversion from the world to God. So too the presence in the world of the church that baptizes in the spirit is the culmination of salvation history. From here on, there is naught to do but wait and watch and pray for the coming end. The church works through her ministers, who attract Augustine's attention a few pages further on:

Now then let Thy ministers work upon the earth, not as upon the waters of infidelity [Gen. 1.2], by preaching and speaking by miracles, and sacraments, and mystic words: with ignorance, the mother of admiration, intent upon them, out of reverence towards those secret signs. Such is the entrance unto the faith for the sons of Adam forgetful of Thee, while they hide from Thy face, becoming a darksome deep. (13.21.30)

This is a world made altogether new by the action of the spirit. Mystery and miracle beget faith, but faith begets faith as well, and the spirit is always present. Mankind is commanded to increase and multiply, by which Augustine understands (13.23.37) no simple command to procreation but a deeper urge to growth and development in the spirit for Christians and for the church. Though sin persists, the spirit creates hope in the place of despair and gives new meaning even to the acts of sinners. This new life of the spirit is a foretaste of what awaits.

The end of the *Confessions* is near, and in a text so emblematic of salvation history as this one, the end of the text will be the end of all things. The six days of creation stand for the whole history of creation. The seventh day is not merely a way of imagining the continued eternal existence of God past the process of creation, but a way of imagining the future for all mankind. The last paragraphs of the work blend theology and prayer in the unique mixture we have learned to recognize as confession:

> O Lord God, give peace to us . . .
> the peace of rest, the peace of the sabbath,
> which hath no evening.
> . . . But the seventh day hath no evening,
> nor hath it setting;
> because Thou hast sanctified it
> to an everlasting continuance. . . .
> That day may the voice of Thy book
> announce beforehand unto us,
> that we also after our works
> (therefore very good,
> because Thou hast given them to us)
> shall rest in Thee also
> in the sabbath of eternal life.
> (13.35.50–36.51)

Salvation history has therefore no end. It ceases to be muddled with actions and distractions, but confession is eternal. This book comes to its last page, but is endless. God continues to work, eternal and never endless.

> But Thou, being the Good which needeth no good,
> art ever at rest,
> because Thy rest is Thou Thyself.
> And what man can teach man to understand this?
> or what angel, an angel?
> or what angel, a man?
> Let it be asked of Thee,
> sought in Thee,
> knocked for at Thee;
> so, so shall it be received,
> so shall it be found,
> so shall it be opened.
>
> (13.38.53)

With these last words we are reminded that the quest is not yet over, that the search is still underway, still beginning anew at each moment. We close the book, in fact, on the Latin word that means "shall be opened." The text is prayer and confession itself, but it is not exclusive. Augustine the writer puts down the pen but does not cease to confess.

Augustine's *Confessions* move from ignorance toward knowledge, both reaching and not reaching that goal. Reaching, in that faith is knowledge; not reaching, in that faith only sees through a glass darkly. The last three books of the *Confessions,* embodying the knowledge of God that Augustine the bishop and author is seen striving for at the end of Book 10, well suit what has gone before.

But there is perhaps one further level of meaning to this peculiar text. Books 11–13 see in God, in the persons of the trinity the qualities of existence, knowledge, and will. We also saw that Augustine elsewhere made much of the parallel that exists between this image of God and the form of human personality itself. The creature exists in the image and likeness of God (Gen. 1.26) and shares in existence, knowledge, and will, insofar as they come from God. Sin is the way men become less like God, redemption the way they come to resemble him again.

There is thus a unique sense in which the last books of the *Confessions* are intimately related to the first ones. The real movement of the *Confessions* is from an initial apparent knowledge of self (and ignorance of God), which then recognizes itself as fraud and ignorance. Augustine moves toward real knowledge of God, in three persons, which is authentic knowledge of self. *Noverim me, noverim te* again: I can only know myself if I know God; to seek to know myself in isolation is the folly of sin.

The first ten books dismantle the apparent knowledge of self with which the sinful Augustine began. In those books, by a negative path, Augustine comes to know himself. Real uncertainty remains, as is clear from the passage in Book 10 where the saintly bishop admits he does not know to which temptation he might next submit.

Books 11 to 13 become more positive. By depicting God through scripture, Augustine is giving the final, authentic depiction of himself. Augustine sees himself not as a unique and interesting sinner (for sinners are neither unique nor interesting), but as a being created in the image and likeness of God. By describing that God, he describes himself now more accurately than he could ever have done before. He describes others as well, for saints resemble each other, despite the uniqueness of personality.

The *Confessions* depict in the end the Augustine with which the work began, but do so with an authority that was lacking at the outset. What sets this pilgrimage apart is that it makes the result a living possibility for every reader. The conclusion—knowledge of God leading to knowledge of self—is one that is accessible to all.

The *Confessions,* then, contain two books. One is the book Augustine wrote. As such it is itself an act of prayer and confession. But the other is the book that every reader takes up, with two possible readings of the book to consider. We may read the text in a detached, anthropological temper, treating it as a historical artifact of late antiquity, a window through which to catch something of the life of that alien time. We may accordingly study the author and his intentions in writing the text. When we do this, however, we are not reading the text Augustine would have us read, and the difficulties modern scholars experience with this text are the result of their professional insistence on giving this text a reading it was never meant to have.

Augustine would never have wanted the text to be anything other than prayer and confession for anyone. By leading in the last books to the abstract and difficult discussion of the trinity and its image in man, he makes it possible for every reader to duplicate the process through which he has gone, to go through that process for himself. The very difficulty of the text thwarts analytic detachment and hurries the reader along. Read in this way, the book is no longer

Augustine's book, but our own book. The creature in the image and likeness of God whom we learn to know from the last books is no longer Augustine (as it was for the author of the text), but ourselves, creatures like Augustine.

Read in this way, this text itself becomes a medium by which we may look past the individual conditions of author–intention–text to a general truth. This work refuses to be an icon for veneration and study in itself. The author himself declines to accept our veneration. Rather, both conspire to pass our attention along imperceptibly to the God that both represent. Ultimately text and author efface themselves, the reader closes the book, and the whole process begins anew. The real book is opened, as the last words of the *Confessions* indicate.

Chapter Six
Reconsiderations

"From his writings it is clear how this bishop beloved by God lived his life, as far as the light of truth was granted him, in the faith, hope, and charity of the catholic church, and those who read what he has written about the things of God can profit thereby. But I think that those who could hear and see him speaking before them in the church could profit more from him, especially those who knew how he lived among men."[1] So wrote Augustine's friend and biographer, Possidius, not long after the old bishop died (28 August 430). He felt what every reader of Augustine has known, the inadequacy of trying to hear the message of this man through the written word alone. Every powerful writer is doomed in this way to outlive his own grave, and to suffer the transformations and deformations that later generations impose on one who is no longer able to protest aloud.

For fifteen and a half centuries, Augustine's words have gone on being read and misread, gone on fueling controversy and lending comfort. Whatever those words meant in his lifetime, and whatever their role in the controversies of the day, they have meant more and exercised more influence since their author's death than before. The history of Augustine's posthumous readership is a part of any attempt to grasp the character of his thought.

Augustine's own last contributions played an important role in shaping and directing posterity's judgment of him. Augustine had lived long enough to see optimistic phrases of his youth thrown up in his face by the Pelagians and their allies. He felt deeply the gaps that separated past from present and present from future. We have seen how the "historical" part of the *Confessions,* the painstaking archaeological excavation of his own past, was meant to put that past to rest and in so doing to clear the stage for what would follow. For Augustine, all human life is preface to a future the human imagination can scarcely grasp; so at every point, the whole past becomes preface anew and the future, whole and entire, remains.

Because Augustine continued to grasp the freshness of the future and refused to accept the finality of the past, he maintained with surprising vitality in old age not only the convictions that had fired him in the fervor of conversion, but even the tenacious power to explore their implications further. This attitude produced what deserves to be recognized as the first work in the history of Augustinian scholarship: it is a book called *Retractationes* (in English, best perhaps as *Reconsiderations*).

In 427, Augustine reopened the excavation into his own past, in a way almost as remarkable as that which produced the *Confessions:* he set out to catalogue his own works, part of a project that was to include a complete register of his letters and sermons as well as his formal literary products. Only the first stage of the catalogue was completed in the form of the *Reconsiderations* we have, but it is to that work, along with an index compiled by Possidius shortly afterwards, that we owe not only our knowledge of the identity and scope of Augustine's works, but even to some extent the very survival of those works. No other ancient author came equipped with so detailed a list of his works for medieval scholars to use in searching out copies with which to supply their libraries. The works had therefore a better chance of survival.

But Augustine was not content merely to catalogue the past. He also reviewed it. For every work listed, he says something of the circumstances of composition and publication and adds something of the corrections and amendments that, in his old age, he found necessary. A fair number of these alterations treat points that had come into controversy since the rise of the Pelagian movement, but the corrections are scarcely limited to such clarifications.

The *Reconsiderations* offer a final open chapter in an intellectual autobiography: "The reader who reads my works in the order in which they were written may learn something of how I progressed as I wrote them."[2] The ideas and themes of Augustine's past literary works were not for him dead accomplishments of his past, but living testimonies to faith. As such they were subject to change and improvement as much as he was. The *Reconsiderations* retroactively turn every one of Augustine's works into a kind of preface of its own. What is important is not that the works were written at some dead time in the past, but that they continued to be read. What matters is not his achievement in writing the works, but the reader's enlightenment on encountering them. To that end, improvement, revision, clarification, and correction all had a role to play. Confession and reconsideration go hand in hand.

The old Augustine observing the young Augustine at a distance, qualifying and rephrasing but for the most part affirming: he is not a bad model for his later students to follow. Not all of his readers have been so indulgent of his faults, though to be sure not all have been so cautiously attentive to the nuances of what he said.[3]

Augustine's death did not transform his readers overnight from partisans to scholars. The debates that had begun over grace and freedom in his lifetime lingered, to divide and embarrass his followers. He was defended, vociferously—perhaps too vociferously, against the criticisms of the Gaulish monks, by Prosper of Aquitaine (d. c. 463), but he was also the thinly veiled target of an influential pamphlet, the *Commonitorium* of Vincent of Lerins (d. c. 450), who proclaimed that Christian doctrine consisted in what had been taught "always, everywhere, by everybody"—and hence by implication did not include novel ideas about predestination propagated by African bishops. Behind both these relatively minor figures stood the charismatic and magisterial authority of Augustine's contemporary, John Cassian, a veteran of eastern monastic discipline who had settled in Gaul and wrote two tremendously influential collections of essays on the monastic life, his *Institutes* and his *Conferences;* his authority and his restraint were equally influential in keeping the controversy within remarkable bounds of toleration. Schism was avoided. Eventually the cause of Augustine's doctrine was taken up by the greatest Latin preacher of the early church after Augustine, Caesarius, bishop of Arles (d. 542), who shepherded the bishops of Gaul through an important council at Orange (in 529) at which the essence of the Augustinian doctrine was affirmed even while certain doctrines (particularly that of double predestination) were foresworn without prejudice to the argument whether or not they could be found in the pages of Augustine.[4]

Augustine's reputation for learning and authority was not materially damaged by the controversy. His generation had given the Latin church four remarkable writers—Augustine, Ambrose, Jerome, and Cassian—and there was never any question but that the greatest of these was Augustine. For the Middle Ages, Augustinianism did not consist solely or even primarily of his doctrines of predestination (this is exactly the reverse of what must be said of the modern period); when controversy arose in these matters, his name would be invoked (and there was a particularly lively outbreak in the ninth century[5]), but his influence was sought most eagerly elsewhere.

From the fifth century to the twelfth in the Latin west, the preeminent cultural institution of Christianity was the monastery. In the monasteries of this period Augustine's influence knew its most unchallenged domination. In the sixth century, the Neapolitan monk Eugippius (d. c. 535) put together a huge anthology of excerpts from the writings of Augustine, for those who could not find time for reading all of him.[6] Pope Gregory the Great (d. 604) is in many ways the most Augustinian of theologians, and at the same time the most original of his early disciples: his thirty-five books of commentary on the book of Job (his *Moralia*) are Augustinian in method and style, with few disagreements on points of doctrine but some rather different emphases at the same time.[7] Isidore of Seville (d. 636) made him an authority in Visigothic Spain,[8] and the immensely learned Bede (d. 735), perhaps Augustine's greatest pupil, distinguished the Anglo-Saxon church with a long series of commentaries on scripture.[9]

The reforms of Charlemagne (d. 814) in matters of education and church government expanded the influence of all the great church fathers by improving the facilities for copying and disseminating manuscripts, and by raising the level of teaching in the monastic schools, but did little more for Augustine particularly than continue what had been now a centuries–long tradition. It remained for the schoolmen of the first universities—particularly that of Paris—in the twelfth and thirteenth centuries to find new ways of exploiting the rich vein of Augustine's teaching. In their works we see the beginning of the process of continuous transformation, and even deformation, that has been Augustine's fate since. The monks had not after all been very far from Augustine in the underlying spirit and method with which they approached scripture and its teachings. The new universities, half–drunk with the heady influence of Aristotelian logic, replaced the scriptural commentary with the formal disputation as the chief vehicle of theological argument: though they quoted Augustine with lavish praise[10], their real function was to supplant him. Though he was still the object of great veneration, he was no longer the latest and highest authority.

Veneration is often the subtlest form of betrayal. That Augustine's own teachings were not exactly the same as those of the scholastics

who praised him, imitated him, and betrayed him can be seen in
the later history of medieval theology. Martin Luther came out of
an Augustinian cloister to brandish Augustinian doctrines of predestination in the face of late scholastic churchmen—but it was a
sometime Augustinian monk, Erasmus, who took up the challenge
to debate Luther in the 1520's on precisely the issues of grace and
freedom that had been seemingly put to rest at Orange a millennium
before. (Erasmus also oversaw in the same decade the publication
of the first complete printed edition of Augustine's works.)[11]

From the Reformation dates the beginning of the tendency to
give the name Augustinianism narrowly to a limited body of pessimistic doctrines about grace and freedom. Not surprisingly, the
reputation of Augustine in later centuries often rose and fell according to the reputation of just those particular doctrines. The
Roman church retained an ancestral reverence for his name and
teachings, but found itself increasingly compelled to disown in
controversy specific propositions for which support could be found—
most embarrassingly—in the writings of Augustine himself. The
respectful tone and zeal for harmony that had characterized the
debates of the sixth century was entirely absent in the sixteenth, to
the lasting disadvantage of Augustine's reputation. The Counter-
Reformation marks the decisive ascendancy of the prestige of Aquinas over that of Augustine in the Roman church, a transformation
scarcely imaginable as late as perhaps 1500.

The last great battle over Augustine's heritage among churchmen
was fought in seventeenth-century France. Cornelius Jansen, bishop
of Ypres (d. 1638), wrote a monumental treatise, the *Augustinus,*
published two years after his death, the fruit—he said—of his
having read the entire body of Augustine's works ten times, and
the works on grace and freedom thirty times. His teachings found
fertile ground in an aristocratic enclave of asceticism outside Paris,
the convent of Port-Royal. The austere and rigorous writers of this
school, particularly Antoine Arnauld (d. 1694) and Blaise Pascal
(d. 1662)—especially in his *Provincial Letters,* waged relentless polemical warfare against the latitudinarian teachings of the Jesuits,
in pitched battle for the hearts of the French ruling classes. Papal
condemnation in 1653 and partial capitulation by the Jansenists in
1668 marked the end of this brief flowering of Augustinian passion.[12] It should not be overlooked, however, that the great edition
of Augustine's works by the Benedictines of St. Maur (beginning

in 1672) is owed at least in part to the enthusiasm the Jansenists fostered.

The heat of controversy did not offer much hope of a calm resolution to the question whether a synthesis of predestinarian teaching such as Jansen's could satisfactorily represent Augustine's many-sided character to a modern readership. The fading of ecclesiastical controversy and the rise of critical scholarship in the eighteenth and nineteenth centuries began to create an environment in which such questions could be debated seriously and real progress made. For Augustine's reputation, this was at best a mixed blessing: if the scholastics had replaced obedience with a sometimes faithless veneration, the age of criticism has often accompanied its veneration with suspicion, and old allegiances faded slowly. Catholic scholars were slow to forgive Augustine for the aid and comfort he offered to Luther, but Protestants were no less slow to forgive him for the medieval church and its practices.

In our own time, Augustine is no longer the venerable ancestor looming over every ecclesiastical controversy that he was for so long, and this is almost certainly to his advantage. We are freer than any generation since his own to confront him as he was, to let him speak for himself, and to live out the implications of hearing what he had to say. Little has changed. The future of Augustine's teaching remains exactly what it was when he was alive and writing; his works exalt and exhaust, just as they always have.

Notes and References

For a list of abbreviations used below, see Selected Bibliography, p. 140.

Chapter One

1. Details of Augustine's early life come for the most part from his *Confessions*. On all biographical points, the reader should consult Peter Brown, *Augustine of Hippo* (London, 1967) for documentation and further information.
2. See Henri-Irénée Marrou, *Saint Augustin et la fin de la culture antique* (Paris, 1948).
3. See H. Hagendahl, *Augustine and the Latin Classics* (Göteborg: Acta Universitatis Gothoburgensis, 1967).
4. Our knowledge of Manicheism is in a state of flux; for the state of affairs in Africa see F. Decret, *L'Afrique manichéenne* (Paris: Études augustiniennes, 1978). A recently discovered Greek life of Mani offers exciting new light; see A. Henrichs, "The Cologne Mani Codex Reconsidered," *Harvard Studies in Classical Philology* 83 (1979):339–67; and L. Koenen, "Augustine and Manichaeism in Light of the Cologne Mani Codex," *Illinois Classical Studies* 3 (1978):154–95.
5. Symmachus is more famous as the last public spokesman of paganism in the western Roman empire: J. Matthews, *Western Aristocracies and Imperial Court, A.D. 364–425* (Oxford: Clarendon Press, 1975), 12–17, 205–10.
6. Matthews, *Western Aristocracies*, 56–87.
7. There has been much debate about the composition of the dialogues; see John J. O'Meara, "The Historicity of the Early Dialogues of Saint Augustine," *Vigiliae Christianae* 5 (1951):150–78.
8. Augustine's life as bishop is well portrayed in Frederick Van der Meer, *Augustine the Bishop* (London, 1961).
9. See W. H. C. Frend, *The Donatist Church* (Oxford, 1952).
10. Peter Brown, "Saint Augustine's Attitude to Religious Coercion," *Journal of Roman Studies* 54 (1964):107–16; Robert A. Markus, *"Saeculum": History and Society in the Theology of Saint Augustine* (Cambridge, 1970), 133–53.
11. G. de Plinval, *Pélage: ses écrits, sa vie et sa réforme* (Lausanne: Payot, 1943).

Chapter Two

1. *Conf.* 11.2.2.

2. *De doctrina christiana;* Latin text in *PL* 34; *CCSL* 31; *CSEL* 80; *BA* 11; English translation in *NPNF*, 1st Ser., vol. 2; *FC; Library of Liberal Arts.* Reference in this chapter not otherwise identified are to this work.

3. Cf. O. O'Donovan, "*Usus* and *fruitio* in Augustine, *De doctrina Christiana* I," *Journal of Theological Studies* 33 (1981):361–97.

4. On trinitarian doctrine, see Jaroslav J. Pelikan, *The Christian Tradition: A History of the Development of Doctrine,* vol. 1, *The Emergence of the Catholic Tradition (100–600),* (Chicago, 1971), 172–225; for Augustine, *The Trinity* is central.

5. For a sensitive criticism of Augustine on this point, see John Burnaby, *Amor Dei: A Study of the Religion of Saint Augustine* (London, 1938), 132–35.

6. Digression is a common feature of ancient literature and was considered an aesthetically pleasing adornment. Augustine's work was admired by his contemporaries at least in part for just the digressions we sometimes find distracting. They had a distinct rhetorical function, as in the example discussed in our text. As heirs of medieval scholasticism we hold that the outline of an argument should be visible to a reader so its validity could be tested against the rules of logic; but the ancient world distrusted logic's clever tricks. The effectiveness of language was judged, not according to the simplicity, clarity, and orderliness of the arrangement of the text itself, but according to the effectiveness with which it persuaded the intended audience in the matter at hand.

7. Cf.: "No one doubts we learn more cheerfully through simile and metaphor. What is sought with difficulty is found with more pleasure. . . . The Holy Spirit [has] arranged the holy scriptures so the hunger for truth is satisfied with clear statements while surfeit and tedium are swept away by more obscure passages. Virtually nothing . . . can be gotten from obscure passages that is not found elsewhere in scripture stated in perfectly clear terms" (2.6.8).

8. *Crede ut intellegas:* "Believe so you can understand" is an often-quoted catchphrase of Augustine's: *Treatises on the Gospel of John* 29.6; cf. *The Trinity* 8.5.8. See André Mandouze, *Saint Augustin* (Paris, 1968), 265–88, and compare the text of Isaiah 7.9 discussed at note 13, chap. 2, below.

9. The seven stages of wisdom are scriptural: "And there shall rest upon him the spirit of the Lord, the spirit of *wisdom* and *purity of heart,* the spirit of *good counsel* and *strength,* the spirit of *knowledge* and loyal *obedience;* and his heart will be filled with the spirit of the *fear of the Lord*"

(Isaiah 11.2, for which Augustine's text differs slightly from modern editions).

10. On the early history of the Bible in Christianity, see the *Cambridge History of the Bible*, vol. 1 (Cambridge: Cambridge University Press, 1970), esp. 67–158, 232–307.

11. Jerome, *Liber interpretationis hebraicorum nominum, PL,* 23.771– 858 and *CCSL* 72.57–161.

12. For the most part, the pre-Vulgate Latin versions have been lost and are being reconstructed by the *Vetus Latina* project of Beuron Abbey in Germany; see the *Cambridge History of the Bible* 1.541–562, and A. M. La Bonnardière, *Biblia Augustiniana* (Paris: Études augustiniennes, 1960–), which will eventually comprise volumes cataloging all of Augustine's own citations of scripture.

13. Augustine cites (2.12.17) a good example in the passage at Isaiah 7.9, where the Septuagint and early Latin translators read, "If you do not have faith, you will not have understanding," a theologically useful proof text (compare note 8, chap. 2, above), much more valuable than the philologically more accurate Vulgate, "Unless you have faith, you will not be established." Eriugena in the ninth century and Anselm in the eleventh had no qualms about preferring the older version. The irony is that modern Hebrew scholarship now discovers that the Septuagint may merely have been making explicit what the Hebrew was saying figuratively.

14. Cf. Henri de Lubac, *Exégèse Médiévale* (Paris, 1959–1964), passim.

15. The earliest heresy, Marcionism, had challenged the use of the Old Testament; it may have been the decisive factor in propelling the orthodox churches to define their canons of received scriptural books. On Origen, see *The Cambridge History of the Bible* 1.454–488.

16. Cf. J. Pépin, *Mythe et allégorie* (Paris: Études augustiniennes, 1958; 2d. ed., 1976).

17. See also 3.2.2 and cf. Book 12 of the *Confessions*.

18. An edition with translation and notes of Book 4 exists, by T. Sullivan (Washington, D.C.: Catholic University of America Press, 1950).

19. See Cicero, *Orator,* 76–99, on the three styles; and cf. E. Auerbach, *Mimesis* (Princeton: Princeton University Press, 1953), esp. 72–73.

Chapter Three

1. *De civitate Dei (City of God);* Latin text in *CCSL* 47–48; reprinted in *BA* 33–37, with much helpful annotation; also in *CSEL* 40; translated by M. Dods (in the *Modern Library*), H. Bettenson (Penguin paperback), G. E. McCracken et al. (*Loeb Classical Library,* with Latin text, seven volumes), J. Healey *(Everyman Library),* and D. Zema et al. *(Fathers of the Church,* three volumes).

2. *Aeneid* 1.278–79: Jupiter: "I set no times or bounds for them; I have granted them empire without end." See Charles Norris Cochrane, *Christianity and Classical Culture* (Oxford, 1942), 62–73.

3. See A. H. Armstrong, ed., *The Cambridge History of Later Greek and Early Medieval Philosophy* (Cambridge: Cambridge University Press, 1967).

4. For his continued hesitation at the end of his life, see *Reconsiderations* 1.1.3; Eugene Portalié, *A Guide to the Thought of Saint Augustine* (Chicago, 1960), 148–50.

5. Cf. A. Lauras and H. Rondet, "Le thème des deux cités dans l'oeuvre de saint Augustin," *Études augustiniennes* (Paris: Aubier, 1953), 97–160.

6. *City of God,* 11.26–28; the same psychology pervades Augustine's writings and is expounded in *The Trinity,* where the three parts of the soul are interpreted as the image and likeness of the trinity in man. Cf. M. Schmaus, *Die psychologische Trinitätslehre des hl. Augustinus* (Münster: Aschendorff, 1927).

7. Cf. Brown, *Augustine of Hippo,* 387–91; J. N. D. Kelly, *Jerome* (London: Duckworth, 1975), 179–86.

8. Cf. Cochrane, *Christianity and Classical Culture,* esp. 336–37.

9. As he did in *City of God* 5.26, a passage that has drawn criticism from modern writers; but cf. Y.-M. Duval, "L'éloge de Theodose dans la 'Cité de Dieu' (V, 26, 1)," *Recherches augustiniennes* 4 (1966):135–79.

10. *The Seven Books of History against the Pagans,* translated in *FC* by R. J. Deferrari. See T. E. Mommsen, "Orosius and Augustine" in his *Medieval and Renaissance Studies* (Ithaca: Cornell University Press, 1959), 325–48.

11. Cf. H.-X. Arquillière, *L'augustinisme politique* (Paris: Vrin, 1934; 2d. ed., 1952).

12. For text, translation, and commentary of Book 19, see R. H. Barrow, *An Introduction to Saint Augustine: "The City of God"* (London: Faber & Faber, 1950).

13. For Augustine's reaction, see the *Life* by his disciple Possidius, chap. 30 (translated in F. R. Hoare, *The Western Fathers* [New York: Harper, 1954], and elsewhere).

Chapter Four

1. On Pelagius, see G. De Plinval, *Pélage, ses écrits, sa vie et sa réforme,* supplemented by R. F. Evans, *Pelagius: Inquiries and Reappraisals* (New York: Seabury, 1968). Pelagius may not have been the originator of the ideas he preached, but he was a useful lightning rod for controversy.

2. *De meritis et remissione peccatorum et de baptismo parvulorum (The Guilt and Remission of Sin; and Infant Baptism):* Latin text in *PL* 44.109, *CSEL* 60; English translation in *NPNF,* 1st ser., vol. 5. The introduction and notes to this volume of *NPNF* are perhaps the handiest detailed discussion of Augustine's side of the Pelagian controversy in English, but must be supplemented with the works cited above and preferably with Peter Brown's able chapters (*Augustine of Hippo,* 353–64, 381–407).

3. See *Conf.* 1.7.11, where he echoes Job 14.4–5 (according an old version): "No one is clean of sin before you, not even the infant whose life on earth is one day old."

4. Augustine's *Baptism* in seven books expounded the theology of the sacrament against the background of the Donatist controversy and the writings of the third-century bishop of Carthage, Cyprian.

5. One other case may be mentioned. In a refutation of Pelagius written in 413–15, *Nature and Grace,* Augustine is at pains to insist that none of the patriarchs and prophets, not even those who were around Jesus in his infancy, were free of sin. But then he adds: "We except the holy Virgin Mary, concerning whom I wish to raise no question when it touches the subject of sin, out of honor for the Lord. From Him we know what abundance of grace for overcoming sin in every particular was conferred upon her who had the merit to conceive and bear Him who undoubtedly had not sin" (*Nature and Grace* 36.42).

6. *De spiritu et littera (Spirit and Letter):* Latin text in *PL* 44, *CSEL* 60; English translation in *NPNF,* 1st ser., vol. 5; *Basic Writings of Saint Augustine,* ed. Whitney J. Oates (New York: Random House, 1948), vol. 1; *Augustine: Later Works,* ed. John Burnaby, vol. 8 of the *Library of Christian Classics* (Philadelphia: Westminster, 1955).

7. For a refutation of the Pelagian system in its fully developed and accurately presented form, see *The Grace of Christ and Original Sin* (from 418; translated in *NPNF,* 1st ser., vol. 5).

8. *Against Julian* 3.10.22.

9. Rom. 11.33–36 or part thereof had appeared at the end of the discussion of grace in Romans at *Seven Various Questions for Simplicianus* 1.2.22; it also appears in at least the following anti-Pelagian works: *Guilt and Remission of Sins* 1.29; *Spirit and Letter* 60 and 66; *Refutation of Two Pelagian Letters* 4.16; *Grace and Free Will* 44; *Punishment and Grace* 17–19; *The Predestination of the Blessed* 4 and 16; *The Gift of Perseverance* 30.

10. *De praedestinatione sanctorum (The Predestination of the Blessed):* Latin text in *PL* 44; *BA* 24; English translation in *Basic Writings,* ed. Oates, vol. 1; *NPNF,* 1st ser., vol. 5.

11. See Pelikan, *The Emergence of the Catholic Tradition,* 319–31.

12. On this, see J. M. Rist, "Augustine on Free Will and Predestination," *Journal of Theological Studies*, 20 (1969):420–47.

Chapter Five

1. *Confessiones (Confessions):* best Latin text by Skutella (Leipzig: B. G. Teubner, 1935; reprint, Stuttgart: B. G. Teubner, 1969), reprinted in *BA* 13–14 with French translation and excellent notes; see also *PL, CSEL, CCSL, Loeb Classical Library* with translation; Latin text with useful English notes by J. Gibb and W. Montgomery (Cambridge 1908, 2d. ed. 1927; reprint, New York, 1979). The classic English translation is that of E. B. Pusey, which is the basis for the quotations here; but I have retouched the quotations occasionally in the interests of accuracy and intelligibility. Italicized words in quotations mark Augustine's (usually unattributed) quotations of scripture.

2. *Soliloquies* 2.1.1.

3. These works were not without occasional suggestive personal notes. Cf. *The Trinity* 15.28.51, the last paragraph of that work, with its reflection on the alarming implications, for a writer as prolific as Augustine, of Prov. 10.19, "You shall not avoid sin by pouring out a multitude of words."

4. See M. Verheijen, *Eloquentia Pedisequa* (Nijmegen: Decker & Van de Vegt, 1949).

5. Rom. 10.14 (abbreviated), Ps. 21(22).27, and Mt. 7.7.

6. The landmarks in this century are the stimulating but finally confounded thesis of P. Alfaric, *L'évolution intellectuelle de saint Augustin: I. Du manichéisme au neoplatonisme* (Paris: Nourry, 1918), and the two masterworks of Pierre Courcelle, *Recherches sur les "Confessions" de saint Augustin* (Paris, 1950; 2d. ed., 1968) and *Les "Confessions" de saint Augustin dans la tradition littéraire* (Paris, 1963). The best summary of the issues in English is John J. O'Meara, *The Young Augustine* (London, 1954; reprint, 1980). My own views would be regarded by all those writers as conservative; I hope to explore them at length in another work.

7. See Courcelle, *Recherches*, 157–67, the classic essay in a long debate.

8. A. Pincherle, *La formazione teologica de Sant'Agostino* (Rome: Edizioni Italiane, 1947) is the best survey of this period, though investigations have continued, e.g., O. du Roy, *L'intelligence de la foi en la Trinité selon saint Augustin: Genèse de sa théologie trinitaire jusqu'en 391* (Paris: Études augustiniennes, 1966). For a concise survey see E. TeSelle, *Augustine the Theologian* (New York: Herder, 1970), 90–182.

9. The best concise view of the Christian Platonists of Milan is in the note by A. Solignac in the second volume of the *BA* edition of the *Confessions*, 529–36.

10. On Victorinus, see P. Hadot, *Marius Victorinus: Recherches sur sa vie et ses oeuvres* (Paris: Études augustiniennes, 1971).

11. M. Atkinson, *Plotinus, Ennead V.1* (Oxford: Oxford University Press, 1983) offers translation and commentary of a Plotinian text Augustine had read on the three hypostases.

12. The stylistic independence of Augustine is well illustrated by the opening words of 8.2.4, which may stand for many similar passages in the *Confessions.* "O Lord, Lord, *Which hast bowed the heavens and come down, touched the mountains and they did smoke,* by what means didst Thou convey Thyself into that breast?" The question is simplicity itself, but the interposed quotation from Ps. 143(144).5 puzzles and repays attention. From Augustine's great collection of sermons on the Psalms, we find that those lines had a particular allegorical meaning for him. (*En. Ps.* 143.12): The "mountains" of the text are the proud men of earth, whom God has to purify of their pride, while the "heavens" stand for the Apostles, the living instruments by which heavenly truth is brought down to earth. Given those equivalences, Augustine says in his sermon that this text summarizes the essential stages of the divine redemption of the individual. Revelation comes through scripture of apostolic origin, and the proud are purged of their sins by the hand of God. On that interpretation the question Augustine asks contains within itself, cryptically, its own answer. The next sentences say that Victorinus studied scripture assiduously and that Simplicianus rebuked his pride and eventually brought him around to accepting church membership along with the most humble. This implicit self-sufficiency of the question is a remarkable sign of the way this text is not meant to be completely self-explanatory to a merely human audience.

13. Burnaby, *Amor Dei,* 210.

14. On this subject, see, P. Henry, *La vision d'Ostie: sa place dans la vie et l'oeuvre de S. Augustin* (Paris: Vrin, 1938).

15. Augustine on prayer: "We might ask . . . what need there is for prayer at all, if God already knows what we need (Mt. 6.8). But the very act of prayer brings serenity to our heart, purges it, and makes it readier to receive the divine gifts that are poured into us of the spirit. Not for the self-seeking of our prayers does God hear them, he who is always ready to give us his light, a light not visible but spiritual and intelligible. It is we who are not always ready to receive it, when we stoop to lowly things and are shadowed over by our lust for material things. In prayer therefore there takes place a conversion of the heart to him who is always ready to give if we but take what he gives, and in that conversion there is cleansing of the inner eye when the material things we crave are shut out. Then the vision of the pure heart can bear the pure light from above that shines without fading or setting. Our heart then can not only bear the light, it can abide in it, not only painlessly but with unspeakable

joy, the joy that brings true and unsullied fulfillment to the blessed life."
(*The Sermon on the Mount* 2.3.14).

    16. See my "Augustine, *Confessiones* 10.1.1–10.4.6," *Augustiniana*
29 (1979):280–303.

    17. K. Grotz, "Die Einheit des 'Confessiones' " (Diss. Tübingen,
1970).

    18. See E. P. Meijering, *Augustin über Schöpfung, Ewigkeit und Zeit*
(Leiden: Brill, 1979).

    19. The only discussion I know of trinitarian patterns in the *Confessions* is H. Kusch, "Trinitarisches in den Büchern 2–4 und 10–13 der
Confessiones," *Festschrift Franz Dornseiff* (Leipzig: Bibliographisches Institut, 1953), 124–83; but my interpretation differs from his at numerous
points.

Chapter Six

    1. Possidius, *Life of Augustine* (see note 13, chap. 3, above), chap.
31.

    2. *Reconsiderations,* Prologue, 3.

    3. The presence of Augustine in later thought and controversy is a
force so powerful that it has defeated modern attempts to capture its story
on paper in brief compass. One way to trace his influence is through the
standard histories of Christian doctrine; see Jaroslav J. Pelikan, *The Christian Tradition: A History of the Development of Doctrine,* vol. 3, *The Growth
of Medieval Theology (600–1300)* (1979), and vol. 4, *Reformation of Church
and Dogma (1300–1700)* (1984). Pierre Courcelle, *Les "Confessions" de Saint
Augustin dans la tradition littéraire* (Paris, 1963), comprehensively outlines
the vicissitudes of readership of that one work. There are in addition
myriad special studies on particular points of influence: the bibliographical
tools listed at the end of the Selected Bibliography can provide guidance.

    4. There is no completely satisfactory work on the Gaulish controversies; beyond the few pages in Pelikan (see note 11, chap. 4 above), the
story emerges best as a subplot in F. Prinz, *Frühes Mönchtum im Frankreich*
(Munich: Oldenbourg, 1965).

    5. Pelikan, *The Growth of Medieval Theology,* 80–95.

    6. Eugippius's *Thesaurus* (never translated: text in *CSEL*) gives a
useful caution against overestimating the influence of Augustine's personality. Where a modern anthology of an ancient writer will concentrate on
what is characteristic of that writer, and on his personal contribution,
Eugippius saw Augustine as a great teacher but as one still subordinate
to a higher authority: his anthology is accordingly arranged to place the
extracts from Augustine as much as possible in the order of the books of
scripture on which they throw light. (The pamphlets on grace and freedom

are very thinly represented in the anthology, tacked on at the end with other works Eugippius obviously thinks are of lesser importance.)

7. English biography of Gregory the Great by J. Richards, *Consul of God* (London: Routledge, 1979); best survey of doctrine by C. Dagens, *Saint Grégoire le Grand: Culture et expérience chrétiennes* (Paris: Études augustiniennes, 1977).

8. J. Fontaine, *Isidore de Séville et la culture classique dans l'Espagne Wisigothique* (Paris: Études augustiniennes, 1959; 2d. ed., 1983).

9. P. Hunter Blair, *The World of Bede* (New York: St. Martin's Press, 1971).

10. The first great textbook of the scholastics was the *Sentences* of Peter Lombard, a collection of quotations to form the basis of debate and research: the first quotation was from Augustine's *Christian Doctrine*.

11. Erasmus and Luther exchanged pamphlets on "Free Will" and "Unfree Will" in 1524; they have been frequently translated and offer a snapshot—but only a snapshot—of the battle over the Augustinian legacy in that period.

12. There are many studies of Port-Royal, but the best survey to situate it in a theological context is Henri de Lubac, *Augustinianism and Modern Theology* (New York: Herder, 1969).

Selected Bibliography

PRIMARY SOURCES

The surviving works of Augustine comprise a little over five million words; a complete edition fills at least a dozen volumes. This list arranges the works by contents, and within each section works are alphabetized. Generally accepted dates of composition are given, but note that for many of the longer works a range of dates is given, signified by two dates connected by a hyphen, while for others whose exact date of composition is not known I give two dates separated by a slash to indicate approximation. (The standard work on the chronology is that of S. Zarb, *Chronologia operum sancti Augustini* [Rome: Pontificium Institutum "Angelicum," 1934], but research has continued apace; see particularly A. M. La Bonnardière, *Recherches de chronologie augustinienne* [Paris: Études augustiniennes, 1965].)

In the following list, the asterisk designates titles for which older English translations exist such as may commonly be found in large libraries, translations currently in print are specified by abbreviations.

> *ACW:*   *Ancient Christian Writers*
> *FC:*   *Fathers of the Church*
> *NPNF:*   *Select Library of Nicene and Post-Nicene Fathers*

Latin texts may be found in the following series (only the first contain all of Augustine's works). To locate texts of all the Latin church fathers, see the *Clavis Patrum Latinorum,* 2d ed., ed. E. Dekkers (Steenbruge [Belgium]: St. Peter's Abbey, 1961).

> *PL:*   *Patrologia Latina*
> *CSEL:*   *Corpus Scriptorum Ecclesiasticorum Latinorum*
> *CCSL:*   *Corpus Christianorum, Series Latina*
> *BA:*   *Bibliothèque Augustinienne* (with excellent annotation and bibliography in French)

1. Early Writings [386–91] (omitting items listed in categories below devoted to specific controversies)

Contra academicos (Against the Academics) [386]. *ACW; FC.* Dialogue in three books refuting the "academic" skepticism of Cicero's followers.

De beata vita (The Happy Life) [386]. *FC.* Philosophical dialogue from Cassiciacum.

De dialectica (Logic), De grammatica (Grammar) [c. 387]. Unfinished parts of an unfulfilled plan to write treatises on the seven liberal arts. Cf. *De musica* below.

De immortalitate animae (The Immortality of the Soul) [387]. *FC.* Sketch for a third book of *Soliloquia.*

De libero arbitrio voluntatis (The Free Choice of the Will) [388–395]. *FC* (also in *Library of Liberal Arts* paperback). Dialogue in three books; philosophical analysis of a problem Augustine would later treat in greater depth, with more reference to scriptural data.

De magistro (The Teacher) [389]. *FC.* Dialogue, on knowledge and its transmission, between Augustine and his natural son Adeodatus shortly before the son's death.

De musica (Music) [387–391?], in six books. *FC.* Deals with abstract questions of time and number and with music treated mainly as a question of rhythm.

De ordine (Order) [386]. *FC.* Dialogue from Cassiciacum on divine providence.

De quantitate animae (The Magnitude of the Soul) [387/8]. *ACW; FC.* Dialogue inquiring into the nature of the soul and its attributes.

De utilitate credendi (The Usefulness of Belief) [391/2], *FC.* An apologetic work written for a man Augustine was attempting to convert to Christianity.

De vera religione (True Religion) [391]. *FC.* General defense of the excellence of Christianity. This is the last of his works from before his ordination and shows his mind on the point of turning to a more ecclesiastical style.

Soliloquia (Soliloquies—a word Augustine coined for this work) [386/87]. A dialogue between "Augustine" and "Reason"; a challenging first statement of themes that recur throughout his career.

2. Scriptural exegesis (The numerous collections of "questions" are extremely various in character.)

Adnotationes in Job (Notes on Job) [399]. Not a commentary, but a series of unconnected notes taken down by Augustine's disciples without his awareness; he was later sorry that so inadequate a work had gotten into circulation.

De consensu evangelistarum (The Harmony of the Evangelists) [400?, or perhaps 400–412], in four books.* Discussion of the "synoptic question" comparing the narratives given in the four gospels.

De diversis quaestionibus LXXXIII (Eighty-three Various Questions) [388–395]. *FC.* Collection of short treatises, many exegetical but some philosophical, on a variety of topics, written at Tagaste and Hippo.

De diversis quaestionibus VII ad Simplicianum (Seven Various Questions for Simplicianus) [395].* Written from Hippo in response to a request from Simplicianus, his friend and counselor during his time in Milan and eventual successor of Ambrose as bishop there. The discussion of grace arising from Paul's letter to the Romans is important.

De genesi ad litteram imperfectus liber (Incomplete Literal Commentary on Genesis) [393/94]. Written after the tract against the Manicheans (see under 3 below); broken off after only 10,000 words or so; to be replaced by:

De genesi ad litteram (Literal Commentary on Genesis) [401–414/415], in twelve books.* The theology of creation, from the first three chapters of Genesis.

De VIII Dulcitii quaestionibus (Eight Questions for Dulcitius) [425/426]. *FC.*

De VIII quaestionibus ex veteri testamento (Eight Questions on the Old Testament) [419?].

De sermone Domini in monte (The Sermon on the Mount) [394]. *FC.*

Enarrationes in Psalmos (Sermons on the Psalms) [392–418].* Treatises, mainly in the form of public sermons, on all 150 Psalms (with a few treated more than once); a rich source of Augustine's spiritual ideas.

Epistulae ad Galatas expositio (Commentary on Galatians) [394/395].

Epistulae ad Romanos inchoata expositio (Incomplete Commentary on Romans) [394/395]. Barely begun.

Expositio LXXXIV propositionum ex epistula ad Romanos (Eighty-four Topics from Paul's Letter to the Romans) [394/395].

Locutiones in Heptateuchum (Figures of Speech from the Heptateuch) [419–420]. On the first seven books of the Old Testament, mainly on obscurities of expression arising from the literal (and sometimes inaccurate) quality of Latin translations of those books.

Quaestiones XVII in Matthaeum (Seventeen Questions Concerning Matthew) [400–410].

Quaestiones in Heptateuchum VII (Seven Questions Concerning the Heptateuch) [419–420].

Quaestiones evangeliorum ex Matthaeo et Luca (Questions Concerning Matthew and Luke) [395–399], in two books.

Sermones (Sermons) [392–430]. Only a few of the more than 300 to survive have been translated.

Speculum (Mirror of Scripture) [427]. Compilation of extracts from scripture.

Tractatus in evangelium Iohannis CXXIV (Treatises on the Gospel of John) [413–418?; the first sixteen sermons may have been given as early

as 406/07, and the whole series may not have been completed until 421]. Complete commentary on the gospel.
Tractatus in Iohannis epistulam ad Parthos X (Treatises on I John) [413?; perhaps 406/07]. Complete commentary on the epistle.

3. Anti-Manichean Writings

Acta contra Felicem Manichaeum (Proceedings against Felix the Manichee) [404?]. Shorthand report of a public debate with one of the Manichean "elect"; cf. the following item.

Acta contra Fortunatum Manichaeum (Proceedings against Fortunatus the Manichee) [392].* Fortunatus was a Manichean priest; his performance in the debate was an unmitigated disaster.

Contra Adimantum (Against Adimantus) [394]. Refutation of the writings of a man said to have been a disciple of Mani.

Contra epistulam Manichaei quam vocant Fundamenti (Against the Manichean Letter They Call "The Foundation") [396].* Detailed refutation of a central Manichean text.

Contra Faustum Manichaeum (Against Faustus the Manichee) [397/98], in thirty-three books (some very brief).* Faustus was a Manichean bishop Augustine had known in his own days in the sect (cf. Book 5 of *Conf.*).

Contra Secundinum Manichaeum, cum epistula eiusdem auctoris (Against the Manichee Secundinus, with a letter by Secundinus) [399]. A polite exchange of letters with one of the Manichean "auditors."

De duabus animabus contra Manichaeos (The "Two Souls," against the Manichees) [392/93].* A discussion of a central Manichean doctrine.

De genesi contra Manichaeos (Commentary on Genesis, against the Manichees) [388/389], in two books. Specialized commentary refuting Manichean doctrines.

De moribus ecclesiae catholicae et de moribus Manichaeorum (The Customs of the Catholic Church and the Customs of the Manichees) [387/389]. *FC.* A general apologetic treatise comparing the two ways of life.

De natura boni contra Manichaeos (The Nature of Good, against the Manichees) [399]. Brief discussion of a central issue.

4. Anti-Donatist Writings

Ad Donatistas post collationem (To the Donatists after the Conference) [413]; see *Breviculus* and *Gesta* below.

Breviculus collationis cum Donatistis (Summary of the Proceedings of the Conference with the Donatists) [412]. A pamphlet to publicize recent events; see *Gesta* below.

Contra Cresconium (Against Cresconius) [405/406], in four books. Cresconius was a learned Donatist layman.

Contra Gaudentium Thamugadensem episcopum Donatistarum (Against Gauden-tius, Donatist Bishop of Timgad) [421/422]. Timgad was a stronghold of Donatism in the mountains of Numidia.

Contra litteras Petiliani Donatistae (Against the Book of Petilian the Donatist) [401/405], in three books. Petilian was Donatist bishop of the important city of Constantine west of Hippo; see *De unico baptismo* below.

Contra epistulam Parmeniani (Against the Letter of Parmenian) [400]. Parmenian was Donatist bishop of Carthage who died c. 392; his pamphlet continued to circulate.

De baptismo contra Donatistas (Baptism, against the Donatists) [401], in seven books.* Refutes the claim of the Donatists that baptism could, and often should, be administered more than once to the same person; important for discussion of the theology of baptism in the African tradition, where it had long been a controversial subject.

De gestis cum Emerito Donatistarum episcopo Caesareae (Debate with Emeritus, Donatist Bishop of Caesarea) [418]. When Augustine visited that city, Emeritus came out of hiding for a public debate.

De unico baptismo contra Petilianum (Single Baptism, against Petilian) [411].

Gesta collationis Carthaginiensis (Proceedings of the Conference of Carthage) [411]. Shorthand report of the climactic debate of June 411. Not strictly a work of Augustine's, but he plays a large part in its pages. Excellent text, translation, and notes in edition of S. Lancel published in the series *Sources Chrétiennes* (1972–1975).

Psalmus contra partem Donati (Psalm against the Donatists) [394]. A summary in easy-to-remember verse of the main points of dispute with the schismatics, meant to reach the widest possible audience. Text in *Revue Bénédictine* 47 (1935):312–30.

5. Anti-Pelagian Writings (Except for the two longer works against Julian [*Contra Iulianum* and *Opus imperfectum*], all of these works are controversial pamphlets.)

Contra duas epistulas Pelagianorum ad Bonifacium Papam (Refutation of Two Pelagian Letters, to Pope Boniface I) [422/423], in four books.*

Contra Iulianum (Against Julian) [423], in six books. FC. Dispute with the young Pelagian bishop of Eclanum (Italy). Cf. *Opus imperfectum* below.

De anima et eius origine [also known as *De natura et origine animae*] *(The Soul and Its Origins)* [420–1].* The origin of the soul was in dispute in connection with the transmission of original sin.

De correptione et gratia (Punishment and Grace) [426]. FC. Deals with the objection that Augustine's view of grace made punishment useless as an instrument of discipline, since salvation is independent of human merit.

De dono perseverantiae (The Gift of Perseverance) [429].* Argues that a moment's grace, without the additional gift of perseverance in grace, is of little avail.

De fide et operibus (Faith and Works) [413]. *FC.*

De gestis Pelagii (The Proceedings against Pelagius) [417].* Interpreting for a Latin audience the synod of Diospolis [415] by which Pelagius had been acquitted.

De gratia Christi et de peccato originali (The Grace of Christ and Original Sin) [418].* The most methodical anti-Pelagian treatise.

De gratia et libero arbitrio (Grace and Free Will) [426]. *FC.* Takes up the theme of predestination.

De natura et gratia (Nature and Grace) [413/415].* The Pelagian position was that man's natural endowments constituted divine grace by themselves.

De nuptiis et concupiscentia (Marriage and Desire) [419/421].* The fruits of original sin to be seen most clearly in the disorders of human sexuality.

De peccatorum meritis et remissione et de baptismo parvulorum (The Guilt and Remission of Sins; and Infant Baptism) [411].* The first anti-Pelagian treatise.

De perfectione iustitiae hominis (The Perfection of Justice in Man) [415].* Can man lead a perfectly blameless life?

De praedestinatione sanctorum (The Predestination of the Blessed) [429].* Augustine's final word.

De spiritu et littera (Spirit and Letter) [412].*

Opus imperfectum contra Iulianum (Unfinished Work against Julian) [429/430].* On Augustine's desk at his death.

6. Pastoral Treatises and Minor Controversial Works

Adversus Iudaeos (Against the Jews) [429/430]. *FC.*

Collatio cum Maximino Arianorum episcopo (Debate with Maximinus, Bishop of the Arians) [427]. Shorthand record of a debate with a churchman who came to Africa with the Arian Vandals.

Contra adversarium legis et prophetarum (Against the Opponent of the Law and the Prophets) [421]. Defense of the Old Testament's place in Christian theology against a recrudescence of one of the earliest heresies, Marcionism.

Contra mendacium (Against Lying) [422]. *FC.* Cf. *De mendacio* below.

Contra Priscillianistas et Origenistas ad Orosium (Against the Priscillianists and Origenists, for Orosius) [415]. A pamphlet on heresies said by Orosius to flourish in Spain. (Cf. H. Chadwick, *Priscillian of Avila* [Oxford: Clarendon Press, 1978]).

Contra sermonem Arianorum (Against a Sermon of the Arians) [419]. Refutation of a pamphlet.

De agone christiano (The Christian Struggle) [396]. Short moral treatise with warnings against various heresies, directed to an unsophisticated audience.

De bono coniugali (The Good of Marriage) [401]. *FC.*

De bono viduitatis (The Good of Widowhood) [414]. *FC.*

De catechizandis rudibus (Instruction of Beginners) [399].* Manual for preachers and catechists.

De coniugiis adulterinis (Adulterous Marriages) [421]. *FC.*

De continentia (Celibacy) [395]. *FC.*

De cura pro mortuis gerenda (The Respect to Be Shown to the Remains of the Dead) [424/425]. *FC.* Deals with the resurrection and the rising vogue of veneration for the relics of the saints.

De divinatione daemonum (The Prophecies of Demons) [406/408]. *FC.*

De fide et symbolo (Faith and the Creed) [393]. *FC.* Expounds the baptismal creed for new Christians.

De fide rerum invisibilium (Faith in Things Unseen) [400?]. *FC.*

De haeresibus (Heresies) [429]. A catalog of errors to avoid.

De mendacio (Lying) [395]. *FC.*

De opere monachorum (The Work of Monks) [401]. *FC.*

De patientia (Patience in the Face of Suffering) [418]. *FC.*

De sancta virginitate (Holy Virginity) [401]. *FC.*

De utilitate ieiunii (The Usefulness of Fasting) [399/405]. *FC.*

Enchiridion (Handbook) [423/424]. *ACW; FC.* Brief summary of Christian doctrine.

[Regulae]. There are later monastic rules attributed to Augustine, but just how much goes back to his pen and how much is the result of later compilation and abridgment is very controversial.

7. Miscellaneous

Confessiones [397(–401?)]. *FC.*

De civitate Dei (City of God) [413–426/427]. *FC.*

De doctrina christiana (Christian Doctrine) [books 1–3, 396/397; book 4, 426]. *FC.*

De trinitate (The Trinity) [399/400–416/421]. *FC.*

Epistulae (Letters), [386–430]. *FC.* About three hundred survive, including twenty-nine recently discovered and published in *CSEL* in 1981.

Retractationes (Reconsiderations) [426–427]. *FC.* A catalog of Augustine's works, with corrigenda noted.

SECONDARY SOURCES

1. Biographical and Historical

Brown, Peter. *Augustine of Hippo.* London and Berkeley: Faber & Faber/ University of California Press, 1967. Lucid, universally acclaimed biography.

Cochrane, Charles Norris. *Christianity and Classical Culture.* Oxford: Oxford University Press, 1942. Interprets the transformation of traditional Roman ideas under the impact of Christianity.

Frend, W. H. C. *The Donatist Church.* Oxford: Clarendon Press, 1952. Standard work on the African churches and their controversies in the age of Augustine.

O'Meara, John J. *The Young Augustine.* London: Longmans, 1954. Biography to the time of his conversion.

Van der Meer, Frederick. *Augustine the Bishop.* London: Sheed & Ward, 1961. Description of Augustine's everyday life and activity in the African church.

2. Christian Doctrine, Theology, and Exegesis

Burnaby, John. *Amor Dei: A Study of the Religion of Saint Augustine.* London: Hodder & Stoughton, 1938.

Butler, Cuthbert. *Western Mysticism.* New York: Dutton 1924; 3d. ed., 1951. Considers Augustine along with Gregory the Great and Bernard of Clairvaux.

Gilson, Étienne. *The Christian Philosophy of Saint Augustine.* New York: Knopf, 1960. Outline of philosophical issues in Augustine's teaching.

Lubac, Henri de. *Exégèse Médiévale.* Paris: Aubier, 1959–1964. The standard work on early Christian and medieval study of the Bible, with much to say on Augustine.

Mandouze, André. *Saint Augustin: L'Aventure de la raison et de la grâce.* Paris: Études augustiniennes, 1968. Evolution of Augustine's doctrines in biographical context.

Margerie, Bertrand de. *Introduction à l'histoire de l'exégèse: III, Saint Augustin.* Paris: Cerf, 1983. Sketches Augustine's principles and practice.

Marrou, Henri-Irénée. *Saint Augustin et la fin de la culture antique.* Paris: Boccard, 1948. Detailed study of the educational and cultural background from which Augustine came and the use he made of his traditions.

Pelikan, Jaroslav J. *The Christian Tradition: A History of the Development of Doctrine. Vol. I, The Emergence of the Catholic Tradition (100–600).* Chicago: University of Chicago Press, 1971. The new standard work on the history of Christian doctrine. Note especially chapter 6, "Nature and Grace."

Portalié, Eugene. *A Guide to the Thought of Saint Augustine.* Chicago: Regnery, 1960. Originally an encyclopedia article in French (1923), in book form this work is the most accessible, best indexed guide to

Augustine's ideas on particular points of doctrine; now out of date but not really superseded.

Rist, J. M. "Augustine on Free Will and Predestination." *Journal of Theological Studies* 20 (1969):420–47. The clearest statement in English of a persuasive contemporary interpretation of the most difficult issues; should be read in connection with Pelikan and Portalié.

TeSelle, Eugene. *Augustine the Theologian*. New York: Herder, 1970. Study of principal doctrines and controversies in biographical setting.

3. Christianity and Society

Brown, Peter. *Religion and Society in the Age of Saint Augustine*. London: Faber & Faber, 1971. Collection of important articles on various subjects.

Cranz, F. Edward. "*De civitate Dei*, XV, 2, and Augustine's Idea of the Christian Society." *Speculum* 25 (1950):215–25.

Deane, Herbert. *The Political and Social Ideas of Saint Augustine*. New York: Columbia University Press, 1963.

Ladner, Gerhard. *The Idea of Reform*. Cambridge, Mass.: Harvard University Press, 1959. Comparative study of several patristic writers.

Markus, Robert A. "*Saeculum*": *History and Society in the Theology of Saint Augustine*. Cambridge: Cambridge University Press, 1970. The standard work on *City of God* and its meaning.

Marrou, Henri-Irénée. *Time and Timeliness*. New York: Sheed & Ward, 1969. Philosophical essay on the meaning of history in the Augustinian spirit.

4. *Confessions* (see also biographies above)

Courcelle, Pierre. *Les "Confessions" de S. Augustin dans la tradition littéraire*. Paris: Études augustiniennes, 1963. Discusses both the sources and the influence of Augustine's masterpiece.

———. *Recherches sur les "Confessions" de S. Augustin*. Paris: Boccard, 1950; 2d. ed., 1968. Biographical inquiries, with particular emphasis on the influence of Neoplatonism.

Guardini, Romano. *The Conversion of Augustine*. London: Sands, 1960. Lucid study with emphasis on theology.

Knauer, G. N. *Psalmenzitate in Augustins Konfessionen*. Göttingen: Vandenhoeck & Ruprecht, 1955. Detailed and fruitful study of the presence of the biblical texts in the *Confessions*.

5. For further bibliography

Augustinus-Lexikon. Basel/Stuttgart: Schwabe, 1985–. When completed, this will comprise four large volumes of encyclopedia-style articles on Augustine's life, works, and doctrines; it should be the standard reference for some time to come.

Fichier Augustinien. Boston: G. K. Hall, 1972–. Comprehensive to 1970 in first series, with one supplement volume (1978) so far published.

Revue des études augustiniennes. Paris, 1956–. Annual survey of books and articles worldwide.

Index

Abel, 56
Academics, 44, 91
Adam, 51, 54, 62, 63, 72, 79
Adeodatus, 3
Africa, 1, 11
Alaric, 11
allegory, 31–32, 57
Alypius, 98, 101, 102
Ambrose, 6, 7, 31, 94, 96, 98, 126
angels, 20, 51–52
Annaba (ancient Hippo), 1
Anthony, 98, 99, 101
Apostles' Creed, 16
Apuleius, 2
Aquinas, Thomas, 128
Aristotle, 23, 127
Arnauld, Antoine, 128
assurance, no doctrine of, 66, 77–78, 111–12, 122
Athanasius of Alexandria, 99, 110
Augustine: born, 2; biographical sketch, 1–13; dies, 124

WORKS:
Christian Doctrine, 14–38, 39, 51, 52, 57, 81, 83, 95, 96
City of God, 12, 42–60, 61, 62, 63, 66; structure (chart), 45
Confessions, 38, 42, 81–123
Figures of Speech from the Heptateuch, 30
The Gift of Perseverance, 77
The Guilt and Remission of Sin; and Infant Baptism, 62–67, 69
Literal Commentary on Genesis, 115
The Predestination of the Blessed, 62, 74–79
Reconsiderations, 125
Seven Various Questions for Simplicianus, 61
Spirit and Letter, 62, 67–74

Ausonius, 5
authority and revelation, 87
autobiography, 83, 104

Babel, 47
Babylon, earthly, 58

baptism, 7, 16, 64–65, 88, 91, 95, 102
Bede the Venerable, 127
Benedictines of St. Maur, 128
Berber language, 1
Bible: apocryphal books, 28; *Itala* (early Latin translation), 29; New Testament, 31, 34, 60–61; Old Testament, 28, 31, 32, 34, 56, 60–61; Septuagint (early Greek translation), 28, 29; Song of Songs, 27; Vulgate (Latin translation mainly by Jerome), 29
Birmingham, 103
bishopric and episcopal office, 8, 14, 16, 80, 92, 93, 95, 104, 105, 109, 110, 111, 114, 121, 122
Buttercup, Little, 39
Byzantium, 43

Caelestius, 12
Caesarius of Arles, 126
Cain, 56
Calvinism, 99
caritas, 24–25, 27, 33, 77, 78, 88, 107
Carthage, 1, 2, 3, 4–5, 9, 11, 44
Cassian, John, 126
Cassiciacum, 6, 92, 93, 102
Charlemagne, 127
Christ, 112, and *passim*
Christianity, *passim*
"Christian society," 40
Cicero, 3, 58, 93; *Hortensius,* 3, 90; *Republic,* 44
civitates, 52
compunction, 101, 111
concupiscence, 53, 65, 110–11
confession (prayer and praise), 83–84, 105–108, 121, 122
Constantine, Roman emperor, 64
Constantinople, Council of (381), 16
Counter-Reformation, 128
cupiditas, 33, 77, 78
Cynics, 44

Dante, 7, 82, 89
digression, 132
Diocletian, Roman emperor, 9